Natal Astrology:

Progressing the Horoscope

Course 10-2

Natal Astrology, Part 2
Progressing the Horoscope
C. C. Zain

The CofL Press

www.light.org

THIS IS A BROTHERHOOD OF LIGHT BOOK
PUBLISHED BY THE COFL PRESS

Progressing the Horoscope is part two of the tenth in a series of twenty-one courses comprising twenty-three volumes.

Copyright © 2014 by The Church of Light

All rights reserved under International and Pan-American Copyright Conventions. Published in the United States by The Church of Light, Albuquerque, New Mexico.

www.light.org.

The Brotherhood of Light emblem found on the title page of this book is a registered trademark of The Church of Light

Individual chapters originally copyrighted in 1934 by Elbert Benjamine.

ISBN 978-0-87887-510-8

Portions of this book not exceeding a total of 2,000 words may be freely quoted or reprinted without permission, provided credit is given in the following form:

> ...from *Natal Astrology: Progressing the Horoscope* by C. C. Zain, published by The Church of Light.

About this Book

Progressing the Horoscope is part two of course ten in the twenty-one Brotherhoods of Light course series by C. C. Zain on the Hermetic Sciences, Astrology, Alchemy, Tarot, Kabbala, and the Occult. The material in The Brotherhood of Light course books was written in the first half of the twentieth century. Chapters were first issued as individual serial lessons. Ultimately the serials were bound as chapters into twenty-three volumes and are known as the "Twenty-One Courses."

The student format, 8½ x 11 with wide margins, is designed to facilitate study. Study questions, located in an appendix, are designed to facilitate taking a final exam that Church of Light members are entitled to submit.

The birth charts in this book were selected by Elbert Benjamine (C. C. Zain) because they represent notable personalities of his day. Many of these will be unfamiliar to most people today. They are included for the astrological correlations to events mentioned in brief biographies that provide valuable examples.

Recognizing the importance of language, The Church of Light wishes to acknowledge that some of the Brotherhood of Light course books may contain language that is today considered sexist, racist or elitist. As with all great leaders and teachers Elbert Benjamine (pen name C. C. Zain) was a product of his time. The Church of Light is, however, bound to C. C. Zain's request that the material not be altered. Instead he suggests that any new facts or changes be introduced in the form of amendments. For his position on this matter, see the "Preface" in this book.

For additional information about The Church of Light, the publisher of this material, please go to light.org.

Elbert Benjamine (C. C. Zain)
1882-1951
Author of the 210 Brotherhood of Light Lessons in 23 Volumes

C. C. Zain is the pen name used by Elbert Benjamine, the noted astrologer, naturalist and occultist, for those writings done under the aegis of The Brotherhood of Light during the years 1914-1951. This body of knowledge has become known as The Brotherhood of Light Lessons.

Elbert Benjamine was one of the most prolific astrological writers of the 20th century. In addition to the twenty-three volumes of the Brotherhood of Light series published under the penname C. C. Zain, Benjamine also wrote more than fifty books and hundreds of magazine articles. A scholar who mastered every physical science of his time, Benjamine brought the same vigor to his exploration of the metaphysical sciences. Like the writings of Bailey, Blavatsky, Steiner, and Heindl, the works of C. C. Zain (Elbert Benjamine) have impacted the lives of thousands of students of Western Occultism.

Elbert Benjamine was born Benjamin P. Williams in the small town of Adel, Iowa, December 12, 1882. He was a natural psychic and seer. As a youngster his heightened awareness brought him into contact with those who had passed from this plane to the next. In the autumn of 1898, he began his esoteric studies. By 1900 he had contacted The Brotherhood of Light and began serious study of astrology. His father was a doctor and deacon in the Disciples of Christ church in Iowa, where the community strongly disapproved of any interest in astrology and the occult. For this reason, upon moving to Los Angeles, he changed his name to Elbert Benjamine in order to protect his family. In the spring of 1910 he gave his promise to write the Twenty-One Brotherhood of Light Courses covering astrology, alchemy and magic, under the penname of C. C. Zain. From that time until his death in 1951, he devoted his life's energy and personal resources to writing the lessons, and to establishing The Church of Light as a vehicle for disseminating The Brotherhood of Light teachings.

Preface

Religion should give instructions in optimum living. Optimum living embraces more than a few hilarious days, a few enjoyable weeks, or a few years of health and material prosperity which are followed by a long period of illness and misery. Optimum living gets the best out of life relative to its entire span. Considering the tremendous accumulation of scientific evidence that life persists after the dissolution of the physical, religion must embrace both life on earth and life beyond the tomb.

For living to best advantage after life on earth is done man must know as much as possible about the inner plane realm, about its energies and properties. And it is becoming increasingly evident that for him to live to best advantage while still in the physical form he must know as much as possible about these inner plane energies.

University scientists have demonstrated extrasensory perception. Man's soul often acquires information, usually unknown to himself, upon which he acts successfully to adapt himself to future conditions he could not have perceived through his reason and physical senses. This extrasensory perception, through which all information must be acquired after he loses his physical body, is equally valuable during and after physical life.

University scientists have also demonstrated psychokinesis. As man will have no physical muscles, and as objects of the inner plane do not respond to gravitation or physical pressure of any kind; after leaving the physical, to move or build anything, or to go anywhere, man must exercise psychokinesis. While still on earth he often is able to bring psychokinesis into play to heal the sick and amazingly demonstrate other desirable physical conditions. Because of this, the use of psychokinesis on earth is equally as valuable as its use after earthly life is done.

On the inner plane there is no air, no moisture, and no molecular vibrations which constitute heat. Thus after he leaves the physical he is not influenced by physical weather. He is influenced markedly by astrological vibrations, which constitute the inner plane weather. Though he may not be aware of it while on earth, the inner plane weather has as much or more influence over his life as the outer plane weather. Therefore, knowledge of how to forecast these astrological conditions and what precautionary actions should be taken relative to them, is equally important to man in the after earth life as it is while he still occupies a physical form.

Mankind is becoming too well educated to be guided either in religion or in its political views by blind belief in propaganda. More and more it is demanding demonstrated facts from those who advocate some economic or political system. And in due time it will demand demonstrated facts on which to base its religion. In 210 Brotherhood of Light Lessons the writer has striven to set forth as many such significant outer plane and inner plane facts, and the logical inferences to be derived from them, as possible.

The writer believes The Religion of the Stars will be the world religion of the future not merely from the facts and logical inferences presented in these 210 Lessons but because these facts will be supplemented by additional facts as fast as they are discovered and verified. The Religion of the Stars is not a static religion. It will progress as fast as there is progress in demonstrable knowledge.

This writer is not so foolish to believe that what has already been published in the 210 Brotherhood of Light Lessons is the last word, or that no errors have been made in them, or that new demonstrated facts may not make necessary some revision of the ideas there presented. He all too well remembers that when he went to college, the atom of each of the many chemical elements was indivisible, unchangeable and indestructible. Einstein had not yet published his Theory of Relativity. And four things which since his youth have so greatly changed civilization, as yet had no existence: automobiles, airplanes, cinema and radio.

While he is still on earth he will do all in his power to acquire new significant facts and revise the Brotherhood of Light Lessons to include them. When he has passed to the next plane undoubtedly new significant facts will be discovered that should be included in The Religion of the Stars. However, as orthodoxy will certainly try to get sufficient control to slant them into conformity with orthodox opinion, he believes the Brotherhood of Light Lessons as he leaves them should remain unchanged.

It would be unethical for someone to insert opinions or discoveries in these lessons and not take both the credit and the blame for them. The writer does not want the credit for the ideas or the errors of some other person. He asks that the printed pages of each lesson be left as he has last revised it.

However, in reprinting, it is easy to increase any lesson to 36 or 40 or any multiple of four pages. He suggests, therefore, that any errors he has made, or new discoveries, or logical opinions derived from these discoveries, be set forth and elaborated in an appendix following the 32 (original format) pages of the lesson which it is thought should be thus amended. Before this is done the writer of the appendix should submit what he has thus written to The Church of Light Board of Directors and secure their approval. And his name should appear in the appendix as the author of such commentary.

The author of the 210 Brotherhood of Light Lessons desires that they be permanently retained as the Stellarian Beliefs as he has written them up to the date of his physical demise, and that subsequent amendments should be credited to the persons who make them.

C. C. Zain

C. C. Zain
(Elbert Benjamine, 1882-1951)

Written in August, 1951
Los Angeles, California

Table of Contents

About this Book vi

Preface viii

The Hermetic System of Progressions 1

Major Progressions of Sun and Angles 21

Major Progressions of the Moon 41

Major Progressions of the Planets 63

Minor Progressions of Sun and Angles 83

Minor Progressions of Moon and Planets 105

Transits, Revolutions and Cycles 125

Rectifying the Horoscope 147

Study Questions 167

List of Charts

Majors: Birth Chart 1a 23

Majors: Birth Chart 316 24

Majors: Birth Chart 317 43

Majors: Birth Chart 2a 44

Majors: Birth Chart 318 65

Majors: Birth Chart 3a 66

Minors: Birth Chart 317b 86

Minors: Birth Chart 3b 107

Minors: Birth Chart 318b 108

Transits: Birth Chart 317c 126

Transits: Birth Chart 3c 127

Transits: Birth Chart 318c 128

David Belasco 149

List of Calculation Aids

Calculating Progressed Aspects by Logarithms 2

Either Proportion or Logarithms Get Correct Dates. 3

Solving Example 11, Lesson No. 111 by Logarithms. 4

Correcting Ascendant for Latitude of Birth 22

Finding the Declination of Major, Minor or Transit-Progressed
M.C. or Asc. for Any Given Calendar Date. 42

Know Your Inner-Plane Weather in Advance 64

Checking the Rectified Chart For Accuracy 148

Key to Brotherhood of Light Serial Lessons[1]

THREE BRANCHES OF STUDY

COURSE TITLE	COURSE NUMBER	SERIAL LESSON NUMBER
ASTROLOGY		
Astrological Signatures	2	1-5, 20, 21, 46, 47
Spiritual Astrology	7	71-83
Horary Astrology	8	36, 86-92
Natal Astrology (2 books)	10	19, 103-117
Mundane Astrology	13	141-150
Weather Predicting	15	190-196
Stellar Healing	16	197-208
ALCHEMY		
Spiritual Alchemy	3	49-54
Mental Alchemy	9	95-101
Natural Alchemy (2 books)	12	125-140
Occultism Applied	14	151-162
Cosmic Alchemy	17	164-172
Organic Alchemy	19	209-215
Personal Alchemy	21	216-225
MAGIC		
Laws of Occultism	1	39-45
Ancient Masonry	4	6-18
Esoteric Psychology	5	56-67
The Sacred Tarot	6	22-33, 48
Divination & Char. Reading	11	118-124
Imponderable Forces	18	183-189
The Next Life	20	173-182

---

[1] The Brotherhood of Light Lessons were originally published as individual serial lessons and later incorporated into book format.

Chapter 1

The Hermetic System of Progressions

Serial Lesson Number 19
Original Copyright, 1934
Elbert Benjamine
a.k.a. C. C. Zain

Copyright 2014, The Church of Light

Calculating Progressed Aspects by Logarithms

RULE: Find the EGMT Interval from noon the aspect is perfect on the day (Major Progression Date) the ephemeris shows it is completed. Divide the hours by 2 and call this months, and the minutes by 4 and call this days. This gives the calendar interval before or after the Limiting Date of the calendar year corresponding to the Major Progression Date.

Solving Example 1, Lesson No. 113, by Logarithms.

Log. (b)	1.8573	0°	20'	Venus past aspect.
Log. (a)	1.2950	1°	13'	subtract daily motion Venus.
Log. (d)	0.5623	6h	35m	minus EGMT interval

Dividing the 6 by 2 gives 3mo. Dividing the 35 by 4 gives 9d. Thus 3mo 9d is the minus calendar interval.

1922y	3mo	22d	L.D. in calendar year.
	3mo	9d	subtract calendar interval.
1921y	12mo	13d	date Venus sextile Saturn r.

Either Proportion or Logarithms
Get Correct Dates.

It is more convenient to work progressed aspects of Sun, M.C. and Asc. by proportion. But when always using 60' as the yearly progression of the Sun, the date the progressed aspect is perfect may be a few days in error. Thus in the example below the Sun on January 4 is moving 61' instead of 60' per day. Using 61', either by logarithms or by proportion, gives the date the aspect is complete as January 3, 1922. January 6, 1922, however, obtained by using 60' as the yearly progression of the Sun, is precise enough for all practical purposes.

Solving Example 6, Lesson No. 111, by Logarithms

Log. (b)	1.7270	0°	27'	distance Sun must travel.
Log. (a)	1.3730	1°	01'	subtract daily motion Sun.
Log. (d)	.3540	10h	37m	plus EGTM interval.

Dividing the 10 by 2 gives 5 mo. Dividing the 37 by 4 gives 9 days. 5mo 9d is the plus calendar interval

1921y	7mo	24d	L.D. in calendar year.
	5mo	9d	add calendar interval.
1922y	1mo	3d	date Sun semisquare Venus r.

Solving Example 11, Lesson No. 111 by Logarithms.

The gap to be closed by the M.C., and therefore by the Sun, is found as indicated in the lesson. On April 10, 1921, the Sun and Mars are thus 21° 45' apart, and must yet close the 8 to make M.C. opposition Mars p. The daily gain of Sun on Mars, as indicated, is 15 .

Log. (b)	2.2553	0°	8'	Sun must gain to make aspect.
Log. (a)	1.9823	0°	15'	subtract daily gain of Sun.
Log. (d)	.2730	12h	48m	plus EGMT interval.

Dividing the 12 by 2 gives 6mo Dividing the 48 by 4 gives 12d. Thus 6mo 12d is the plus calendar interval.

2035y	2mo	9d	L.D. in calendar year.
	6mo	12d	add calendar interval.
2035y	8mo	21d	date M.C. opposition Mars. p.

4

Chapter 1

The Hermetic System of Progressions

RADITION should never be mistaken for recorded history; yet when properly labeled it is sometimes not without a certain interest. And the tradition is that the system of predicting the probable time of events, here presented, has never been lost to The Brotherhood of Light since the days of Atlantis and Mu.

When the darkness shut down on those ancient lands—so the tradition runs—colonies were established where later were to rise Egypt, India, Crete, Peru, Mexico, China and Chaldea—the seven ancient centers of civilization. THE RELIGION OF THE STARS thus transplanted, though modified by the characteristics of each people through whose hands it passed, has finally reached the present generation.

Natal, as well as the other branches of astrology, was practiced in each of the countries mentioned. But in Chaldea predictions were checked as to accuracy by the Anu-Enlil series of observations extending unbroken for over a thousand years, in which the events as they happened were recorded with the astrological positions which coincided with them. This gave to the Chaldeans unusual precision in predicting the nature and time of events in human life.

The Anu-Enlil series of astrological observations is historical, in the sense that archaeologists have unearthed the clay tablets on which the records were made. But that the Hermetic System was derived from a still more ancient source, and reached us by way of Chaldea, is tradition.

My predecessor, from whom I received the tradition, used the system for twenty years before his passage to the higher plane. In 1902, after trying out all the methods in common usage, I adopted it, and found it most satisfactory in an extensive astrological practice which continued up to May 1915. At that time, having discontinued private astrological practice, I commenced teaching it in the astrological classes held in Los Angeles; and in October 1917, as the Hermetic System of Directions, it was published, and since that date has been in constant use in all B. of L. (now C. of L.) classes, wherever held, and has been tested and adopted by a vast number of astrologers throughout the world.

The Brotherhood of Light Astrological Research Department began in April 1924, to solicit data, and since that time has collected, erected, and progressed according to this Hermetic System, many, many thousands of birth charts to the time of some given event. The Progressed Constants for each of the 160 different diseases considered in Course 16, *Stellar Healing*, for each of the diseases considered in the book, *Body Disease and Its Stellar Treatment*, and for each of the events considered in the book, *When and What Events Will Happen*[1], were ascertained in this manner.

The recurrent plaint of Church of Light teachers, from Miami to Seattle, and from New York to Los Angeles, is that their students are so muddled with a variety of systems that even when they think they are using the Hermetic System, in reality they are clouding their judgment with other factors which, however worthy in their own domain have no place in this method.

Some students also seem to think that when they are conversant with Major Progressions and Transits they have education enough. But no one can have that precision of judgment regarding details which differentiates the first class astrologer from the mediocre, who neglects Minor Progressions. And because they attract into the life the little events, from day to day and week to week, and their influence in the life of oneself and one's friends can thus readily be observed, to become fully conversant with them is even less of a task than to master major progressions.

Set up the birth chart of the people you know. Calculate the major-progressed aspects for each important event they can remember, and observe how it fits in with your theories. Calculate the more important minor-progressed aspects in their charts for a month or two ahead, and make an attempt to tell them the nature of half a dozen little events to come, and their dates. Then check the results. And in a similar manner find out how accurate, both as to the event and its importance, your judgment is when based on transit aspects.

If you follow this plan until you are thoroughly grounded in the system here set forth, and know just what you can, and cannot, do with it, you will become a good astrologer. And after you have reached this point will be time enough for you to branch out and try to discover additional information. In fact, when you have reached this point, you should, by all means, thus endeavor still further to increase the range and scope of your knowledge.

All Unnecessary Factors Should Be Avoided

It is one of the cardinal doctrines of science, applicable to every line of research, that so long as a condition can adequately be explained by factors already recognized, no new factor should be introduced into its explanation. Both in delineating the birth chart, and in its progression, we have held tenaciously to

---

[1] Both books are out of print, see *Astrology: 30 Years Research* by Doris Chase Doane.

this principle, upon which material science has so successfully been able to build its systems.

We are sometimes asked why we neglect the Moon's Nodes, the Part of Fortune, and the Fixed Stars in the birth chart. We do so because, up to date, we have not found any condition in a person's life which could not satisfactorily be explained by the planetary positions without recourse to these other factors. We do not say that these positions have no value; merely that up to the present we have found no need to use them in explaining the conditions and events in people's lives.

Events occur in people's lives which can only be explained adequately through the progressed aspects of the Asc. and M.C. We thus progress them, as presently to be explained, as if they were planets. But in the birth chart we do not calculate aspects to the cusps of any other houses, and do not progress planets to aspects of the cusps of any other houses, nor progress the cusps of any other houses in any way; because so far in our very extensive research work we have found nothing that cannot quite as well be explained without such aspects and progressions.

It should be borne in mind that an individual with active extrasensory perception can take almost any system, however unreliable it may be to others, and get startlingly precise results. What we have striven for in our presentation of the Hermetic System, however, is not a system of divination; but to find and include all the actual astrological energies which have an important bearing upon human life. It may be that there are yet factors which remain undiscovered; but if so we will include them only when, through extensive analysis, we have become fully convinced that only by their use can certain conditions or events be satisfactorily explained or predicted.

Events Are Attracted Only by Unusual Thought-Cell Activities

Events and conditions are attracted into human lives—and into the lives of all other creatures—due to the activities of the thought cells within the astral form. The astral form of every living thing is composed of such cells, which we also commonly refer to as stellar cells, built by the consciousness accompanying experiences.

These stellar cells, the more active of which are organized into the dynamic structures mapped by the planets in the birth chart, have a certain intelligence of their own, and work from the inner plane to attract into the life conditions and events corresponding to the way they feel.

When they receive no additional energy from any source, they have only the amount and kind of activity indicated by the birth chart. It is only when, from some source—astrological vibrations, thought vibrations, or the character vibrations of objects—they receive an additional energy supply that their activity is greater than the normal thus shown.

While the effect of conditioning since birth, and the present facilities of the physical environment must also receive attention, the chief problem in predicting the nature and time of events by natal astrology, therefore, is to ascertain the time when certain groups of stellar cells within the astral body will receive additional energy; and in what volume and in what harmony or discord it will reach them.

Relativity Now Explains How Progressed Aspects Time Energy Releases

Only within the past few years has Einstein's Special Theory of Relativity become almost universally accepted by physicists the world over, and become the foundation of the physics as taught in our universities.

The most essential conception of this special theory of relativity, which is now so widely employed to explain the behavior of high-velocity particles, is the interrelationship between velocity and time. It is held that there is no such thing as absolute time, but that as velocity increases time slows down, until at the velocity of light time comes to a standstill. Conversely, as time speeds up, velocity slows down, until at the time speed with which we are familiar objects tend to move at the velocity physical things are observed to do.

If at the velocity of light time stands still, within a single moment of such slow time an infinite number of events could happen. And in a realm, or condition, where velocities are not so great, but are greater than that of ordinary physical objects, a large number of events can happen in a single moment of this slower time. In our dreams, for instance, and to some people when they are on the verge of dying, there are numerous experiences which in ordinary time would require days or years, compressed into a few minutes of the slower time of this borderline state.

Material science has now proved that the nerve currents are electrical in nature and that man has an electromagnetic form. Electromagnetic waves when radiated move with the velocity of light; but electric currents traveling over wires or over nerves move much slower. In other words, in man's electromagnetic form are velocities greater than those of ordinary physical substance, but which are not so great as the 186,284 miles per second (1942) that light travels.

From what has already been said, it will be apparent that if a clock slows down relative to the velocity it acquires, as consciousness attains higher and higher velocities it will be able to have more and more experience within the space of four minutes of this slowed down time. At a certain velocity, which is well within the limit of what can be expected to occur in man's electromagnetic form, the ratio of the number of experiences in four minutes of slower time, to the number of experiences in the faster time of external life, is 365¼ to 1.

As the ratio of velocities between one electromagnetic region of man's body and his physical existence is 365¼ to 1, the occurrences that took place in a little less than four minutes of this slower Major Progression Time, when expressed in the faster Calendar Time of the external world occupy a duration of 24 hours, and what took place in 24 hours Major Progression Time of the boundary region, when externalized on the physical plane takes 365¼ days of ordinary Calendar Time; that is, what took place in one day in the boundary region, when externalized takes place in one year of the faster physical time.

As the ratio of velocities between another electromagnetic region of man's body and his physical is about 13 to 1, the occurrences that took place in approximately 2 hours of this slower Minor Progression Time, when expressed in the faster Calendar Time of the external world occupy a duration of 24 hours, and what took place in 27.3 days of this Minor Progression Time in the boundary-line region, when externalized on the physical plane takes 365¼ days of ordinary faster Calendar Time; that is, what took place in 27.3 days of this Minor Progression Time takes place in one year of faster physical time.

Progressed aspects indicate time-velocity transformations of energies, released according to the day-year, month-year, or year-year ratio, which bring about structural changes within the astral body. These structural changes enable the stellar cells to receive additional energies from the planets and thus gain the impetus to work, from the inner plane, to bring events of a definite type into the life.

The energy release, as mapped by a progressed planet, is in that compartment and zone of the astral body mapped by the house and sign of the birth chart in which the progressed planet is located. Thus a planet merely moving through a house of the birth chart by Transit, by Minor Progression, or by Major Progression, brings about a structural change in the astral body which enables it to receive energy, of the nature indicated by the progressed planet, in that region. The energy release shown by a progressed planet forms a temporary stellar dynamic structure within the astral body. This acts as a radio receiving terminal for picking up and transmitting to that compartment of the astral body the energies of the vibratory rate of the planet.

Progressed Aspects Build Temporary Stellar Aerials

When such a progressed planet forms an aspect with a planet in the birth chart, or with another major-progressed planet, the energy release builds across the astral body a line which acts as an aerial which picks up and transmits to its two terminals, energy of the types of the two planets involved in the aspect. In our extensive statistical studies we have found that when Mars or the Sun is involved, and at the same time there are other heavy progressed aspects which act as Rallying Forces, the indicated events may occur when the progressed aspect is as much as a degree and a half from perfect. But as a general rule the effective orb within which the event indicated by a progressed aspect may be expected to take place is one degree from the perfect aspect.

Before it reaches one degree from perfect the line across the astral body usually has not become dense enough to act as an effective aerial. But at one degree from perfect it is dense enough to pick up about one half the peak load of the aspect, gradually increasing in power until the peak is reached when the aspect becomes perfect, then decreasing in power until at one degree beyond perfect it picks up only about one-half the peak load, past which point it usually has dissolved so far that it is no longer an effective receiver.

While within one degree of perfect the progressed aspect maps a temporary aerial stretching across the astral body which picks up astral energies from the planets, from the thoughts, and from the character vibrations of objects, which are of the frequency of either planet, and transmits them to the stellar cells mapped in the astral body by these planetary terminals.

These temporary stellar aerials thus formed by the cyclic release of energy, have a length indicated by the aspect which maps them, and this determines whether the astral energy, from any source derived. which they pick up, will be given a harmonious turn, or will be loaded with discordant static.

To the extent they transmit energy which is harmonious to the stellar cells at their terminals, are the thought cells there given impetus to work to attract favorable events. Likewise, to the extent these temporary stellar aerials transmit energy which is discordant to the stellar cells at their terminals, are the thought groups there located given an impetus to attract misfortune.

But in thus considering the type of activity of any group of thought cells in the astral body as accelerated by new energy received, the type of activity they already possess, due to the conditions under which they originally were formed as modified by conditioning since human birth, is fully as great in importance as the quality of the new energy received.

That is, if they are composed of inharmonious thought compounds, as mapped by unfavorable birth-chart aspects, the mere adding to them of a supply of harmonious energy is not sufficient markedly to change their nature. Or if the compound of which they are formed is quite harmonious, as shown by the birth-chart aspects, the mere supplying them temporarily with discordant static does not cause them to feel so intensely malignant that they work to attract misfortune.

Any energy supplied by a temporary stellar aerial is thus of no more importance in determining the amount of harmony or discord which a group of stellar cells feels than are the permanent aerials mapped by aspects in the birth chart.

These permanent stellar aerials, unless changed through the deliberate cultivation of new processes of thought to dissolve them, not only indicate the nature of the thought compounds at their terminals, but they continue to feed them with astral energy of the harmony or discord denoted by the aspects. And because the thought elements in the compounds were originally united as indicated by the aspects, and continue to receive some energy of the same quality, the temporary energy afforded by a less permanent stellar aerial is limited in its power to cause them to act in a manner different than has been their custom.

Importance of Event Depends Upon Intensity of Thought-Cell Activity

In predicting what events will be attracted into the life at a given time, therefore, the first thing to do is to consider the normal composition and activity of the thought cells within the compartment of the astral body affected. Then consider the volume, type, and harmony or discord of the energy added to the stellar cells within the compartment, and estimate not merely the amount of activity which will result from this new energy supply, but also how the new energy supply modifies or accentuates their normal feeling of harmony or discord.

The importance of the event, other things being equal, will be in proportion to the volume of energy received. That is, in the same physical environment it is always in proportion to the amount of thought-cell activity. But the fortune or misfortune of the event—its harmony or discord—cannot be determined solely by the harmony or discord of the energy added. The new energy merely modifies the normal feeling of pleasure or pain of the stellar cells. It does not change them completely. Thus the fortune or misfortune of the event cannot be ascertained merely from the harmony or discord of the progressed aspect in relation to the physical environment, but must be determined from the harmony or discord of the stellar cells made active in relation to the environment.

Because of the smaller volume of energy picked up by their temporary stellar aerials, only events of less importance are attracted by the stellar cell activity indicated by Minor-Progressed aspects and Transit aspects. No event of outstanding importance will be attracted into the life unless there is a much stronger temporary stellar aerial, mapped by a Major-Progressed aspect, within approximately one degree of perfect, stretching across the astral body.

The event attracted by the additional thought-cell activity will, of course, relate to a department of life to which the stellar cells, as mapped by their house position in the birth chart, belong. That is, the event will refer to one or more of the compartments in the astral body which, by house position, the planets involved in the aspect rule. And the circumstances attending the event will be characteristic of these planets.

It is not a difficult matter—because the progressed planetary aspects so reliably indicate the time of formation of temporary stellar aerials across the astral body which pick up and deliver new astral energy to definite groups of stellar cells—accurately to predict about when, and relating to what departments of life, an event will happen. But it is far more difficult to determine its importance, how fortunate or unfortunate it will be, or the specific event.

Determining Harmony or Discord of Thought-Cell Activities

The reason the degree of fortune or misfortune of the event is difficult to determine is not only due to the resistance or facilities which environment offers to bringing about what the thought-cells desire, but also that a variety of conditions may influence the stellar cell activity as to harmony or discord. The normal way the thought cells feel, in the compartment of the astral body influenced, must be estimated. Then must be gauged just how much this normal feeling will, or will not, be changed by the new influx of energy. Furthermore, it must be considered to what extent, if any, Rallying Forces, indicated by other progressed aspects, will be able to reach these stellar cells with their type of energy.

That is, there is always the factor of the general Mental Attitude; because if this, in spite of the particular progressed aspect under consideration, keeps the consciousness tuned in on some other type of feeling, this supplies the stellar cells at the terminals of all stellar aerials with energy of this harmony or discord, and their activities to attract fortune or misfortune are modified accordingly.

The reason progressed aspects usually work out in terms of their own harmony or discord is because few persons resist permitting themselves to think and feel, at such times, that which is indicated. Even the unwitting application of Mental Alchemy or Rallying Forces, as by those who because of their religious convictions or belief in New Thought continue to feel cheerful and happy in spite of apparent adversity, quite markedly, as we have had occasion to observe, modifies the misfortune that otherwise might be expected from a severe progressed aspect.

In other words, what is attracted to the individual is not due to the birth chart or to the progressed aspect, but is due to the activity of the thought cells within the astral body, working from the inner plane. Anything, therefore, which alters this thought-cell activity, from whatever source it comes, or which alters the resistance of the physical environment to that which the thought cells strive to bring to pass, also alters the fortune.

It is because structural changes within the astral body—which as to time and nature can be ascertained by calculating Major Progressions, Minor Progressions and Transits—are commonly the most influential means through which astral energies are added to the stellar cells within the astral body, that these become of utmost importance in every human life.

The positive influences in an individual's life, measuring the releases of energy which bring structural changes in his astral body at times which can be predetermined, that in turn afford certain stellar cells with the energy to attract events, with which an astrologer should concern himself, in addition to the birth chart, are only these three: Major Progressions, Minor Progressions and Transits.

The only difference to be observed in the influence of these three measures of progression is in the relative amount of structural change indicated by each, and consequently the volume of energy afforded the thought cells above their normal amount, which makes the events attracted relatively important or unimportant.

That is, the structural changes indicated by Transits give the thought cells only enough additional energy to attract inconsequential events. The structural changes indicated by Minor Progressions afford the stellar cells enough energy to attract the minor events of life. But it is only the structural changes indicated by Major Progressions which afford the thought cells in any compartment of the astral body with sufficient additional energy that through their inner-plane activities they can attract important events into the life.

Major Progressions

Major progressions are measured by the ratio of the movements of the planets during one apparent solar day releasing energy which causes the chief structural changes within the astral body that take place during one astrological year in the life of man.

This simply means that the movements and positions of the planets each four minutes after birth indicate the structural changes that take place within the astral body each day after birth; that the movements and positions of the planets each two hours after birth spread the structural changes so shown over each month of life after birth and that the movements and positions of the planets each day after birth relate to the structural changes within the astral body that take place during the corresponding year of life. To calculate the time, therefore, when any particular structural change of major importance will take place, is merely a matter of solving a simple problem in proportion.

Up to 1942 it had been the custom to solve the simple problems in proportion involved in ascertaining when given major-progressed aspects would be perfect in the manner still followed in the text of chapters 2, 3 and 4 (Serial Lessons 111-113). But in that year I published the reference book, *Progressed Aspects of Standard Astrology*[2], in which the simple problems in proportion involved in calculating progressed aspects are solved through the use of logarithms.

It should be understood that the precise time a progressed aspect is perfect is exactly the same whether the method of proportion is employed or the method of logarithms. We discover, however, that some students find logarithms easier to use than proportion, while other students find proportion easier. Which is used is quite optional, as the final result is exactly the same.

It will be seen that as a planet's movement between two consecutive noons in the ephemeris is the equivalent of 12 months Calendar Time by major progression, that the planet's movement during 2 hours (12 of 24 hours) is the same as 1/12 of the planet's movement during the same 24 hours. Whether the planet's motion during 24 hours is divided by 12, or its motion during 2 hours is calculated, the result is the same, and in either case represents its travel by major progression during one month of Calendar Time. In other words, it follows from the time-velocity relativity which permits astrological energies to be released by progression, that the position of a progressed planet may be calculated either by its proportional movement through space (as illustrated in the text of the lessons which follow), or by its proportional movement relative to time (which is the method of logarithms).

In placing the planets in the chart of birth when erecting the horoscope it is customary to find the distance that a planet has moved from ephemeris noon position by adding (d) the logarithm of the EGMT Interval, to (a) the logarithm of the daily motion of the planet. The logarithm so found is then (b) the logarithm of the distance the planet has traveled. Therefore, if we wish to know (d) the EGMT Interval it takes a planet to travel (b) a given distance required to complete an aspect, it is obvious we must merely reverse this process, and subtract (a) the logarithm of the daily motion of the planet, from (b) the logarithm of the distance the planet moves.

When the EGMT Interval is thus simply found it may then be converted into Calendar Time Interval according to the time-velocity ratio, which for major progressions is:

24 hours (one day) major progression (ephemeris EGMT Interval) time equal 12 month (one year, or 365¼ days) calendar time.

---

[2] Out of print, see *Astrology: 30 Years Research* by Doris Chase Doane.

2 hours (120 minutes) major progression (ephemeris EGMT Interval) time equal 2/24 years (one month or 30 days) calendar time.

4 minutes (120 minutes divided by 30) major progression (ephemeris EGMT Interval) time equal 1/30 month (one day) calendar time.

Now, as ephemeris EGMT Interval is major progression time which can always be converted into Calendar Time according to the ratio just indicated, the EGMT Interval from noon on the day of birth—for which the distance the planets had traveled from their noon positions were calculated when finding their places in the birth chart—can be converted into Calendar Time. The noon positions of the planets on the day of birth thus represent their progressed positions on a definite calendar date. Mathematically it makes no difference if the calendar date found occurs before the birth of the individual, for in that case we have merely moved back from birth to get a starting point for calculating progressed positions during his life.

It should be obvious that if in placing the planets in the chart of birth we moved them forward from ephemeris noon positions—using a plus EGMT Interval—that to get them back to noon positions we must subtract their movement from their ephemeris positions. Also if we are to ascertain the Calendar Date corresponding by major progression to this moving the planets back to their noon positions, we must move back from birth the calendar interval represented by the EGMT Interval during which the planets thus are moved.

However, if in placing the planets in the chart of birth we moved them back from ephemeris noon positions—using a minus EGMT Interval—to get them again to noon positions we must move them forward their motion during the same EGMT Interval. And if we are to ascertain the Calendar Date corresponding by major progression to this moving the planets ahead to their noon positions, we must move ahead from birth the calendar interval represented by the EGMT Interval during which the planets are thus moved.

Whether the method followed in calculating the progressed aspects is that of proportion or that of logarithms, the calendar date thus found—called the LIMITING DATE—constitutes the most convenient starting point in calendar time. The Limiting Date (L.D.) must include year, month and day of calendar time.

As the positions of the planets in the ephemeris on the day of birth represent their major-progressed positions on the L.D., the positions of the planets in the ephemeris on the day following birth represent their major-progressed positions on the month and day of the L.D. in the following calendar year; each succeeding day in the ephemeris showing the major-progressed positions of the planets on the month and day of the L.D. in the corresponding calendar year.

The ephemeris date which shows the positions of the planets by major progression as they appear for the month and day of a given calendar year is called the Major Progression Date. And for finding it we use the Limiting Date as the base or starting point in calendar time, and the day of birth as the base or starting point which is equivalent to it in progression time. Thus to find the Major Progression Date we merely count ahead in the ephemeris from the day of birth (major progression time) as many days as years of life (calendar time) have elapsed since the Limiting Date.

To find the progressed M.C., add to the birth-chart M.C. the number of degrees and minutes the Sun has progressed since birth. To find the progressed Asc., take a table of houses for the latitude of birth and merely ascertain the degrees and minutes on the Asc. with the progressed M.C. already found. Other progressed house cusps are not wanted, but if they were, they could be taken from the table of houses corresponding to the progressed M.C. and Asc.

The M.C. and Asc. are unique positions, unlike other house cups. The M.C. marks a thin blue line through the astral body which acts as an amplifier; while the Asc. is a heavy line which serves as a ground wire over which electromagnetic energy reaches the outside world. Very extensive experience leads to the conviction that not merely in the birth chart, but also by progression, these two positions act very much after the manner of planets.

In many, many thousands of birth charts with progressed aspects worked out to the time of events handled by our research department, we have never, however, found it necessary to consider aspects to any other house cusps in the birth chart, or to progress the cusps of houses other than the Asc. and M.C.

The house cusps of a birth chart map the dividing membranes between one compartment in the astral body and another. These astral membrances mapped by the house cusps do not act in the manner of planets. Consequently, while we progress the Asc., M.C. and planets through the houses of the birth chart, there is no progressed chart, in the sense of progressing all the house cusps, in the Hermetic System.

We have done a vast amount of research work on progressed aspects, and we find they invariably work out in terms of the houses of the birth chart through which the planets are progressing or which they rule.

The reason the M.C. is progressed the same distance the Sun moves by progression is that this avoids an error, due to the difference between mean time and true or apparent solar time, which is introduced when the progressed M.C. is found by using the mean time of birth on the major progression date.

This discrepancy in extreme instances would cause an error of approximately 7½ degrees in the progressed M.C. and Asc.; which is the equivalent of about

7½ years. But such an error in timing the progressed planets would be less than 8 days. On the average, in calculating progressions for middle life, the discrepancy amounts to, perhaps, 2 to 12 minutes. This would cause an error of from one to three days in timing planetary progressions, which is close enough for practical purposes. But in timing the progressed aspects of the M.C. and Asc., the error would be from one to three years, which cannot be tolerated.

Minor Progressions

Minor progressions are measured by the ratio of the movements of the planets during one astrological month releasing energy which causes the minor structural changes within the astral body that take place during one astrological year in the life of man.

This means that the movements and positions of the planets while the Moon passes through each degree of the zodiac after birth indicate the minor structural changes that take place within the astral body each day after birth; that the movements and positions of the planets while the Moon moves one sign through the zodiac represent the minor structural changes in the astral body during one month of life; and that the movements and positions of the planets while the Moon moves through the whole zodiacal circle indicate the structural changes within the astral body that are spread proportionally over the whole year.

RULE: From the position of the Moon in the zodiac at birth, count ahead in the ephemeris as many astrological months—successive transits of the Moon over the degree and minute of the zodiac it occupied at birth—as there have been completed years of life. The positions of the planets, M.C. and Asc. during the following astrological month will form the Minor Progressions for the year of life following the birthday. The M.C. progresses the same number of degrees that the Sun has progressed by Minor Progression. As the Sun is always the same number of degrees zodiacally from the M.C. as at birth, the M.C. is easily found from the Sun's position by Minor Progression; adding or subtracting from the Sun's minor position its zodiacal distance from the M.C. at birth. The progressed Asc. may be ascertained from a table of houses for the latitude of birth by using the M.C. so found.

The aspects formed by the progression of the planets, M.C. and Asc. at the rate of one astrological month for each year of life, as strictly between Minor-Progressed positions produce imperceptible effects. But when formed between Minor-Progressed planets and angles to the planets and angles of the birth chart, or to the positions of the major-progressed planets and angles, they produce structural changes within the astral body which attract the minor conditions and events of life.

Transits

Transits are measured by the ratio of the movements of the planets during one astrological year releasing energy which causes the inconsequential structural changes within the astral body that take place during one astrological year in the life of man.

This means that the positions of the planets shown in the ephemeris, from day to day, bring about small structural changes in the astral body on those days.

RULE: The transits of the planets through the houses, especially the slower moving planets through angular houses, should be noted. The conjunction aspect of transiting planets with birth-chart or major-progressed planets in particular is worth observing, and next, the oppositions thus made by the slower moving planets. Only the aspects made to birth-chart positions and Major-Progressed positions should be noted; no attention being paid to transiting aspects to Minor-Progressed positions, or to other Transiting positions.

In our very extensive research work we have been unable to notice any difference in the influence exerted by Major-Progressed aspects, Minor-Progressed aspects and Transit aspects, other than the volume of energy supplied the stellar cells as indicated by the importance and magnitude of the event attracted.

The events which many people believe to be occasioned by transiting planets are really coincident with major-progressed aspects which have formed heavier temporary stellar aerials. Under such circumstances the transit, which merely aids the Major Progression, and which fails to work when no such Major-Progressed aspect is present, is often accredited with full responsibility for attracting the event.

Predicting Events

Except when influenced by Rallying Forces, each progressed aspect tends to work out in terms of its own departments of life as indicated by the house rulerships of the planets involved. That is, progressed aspects do not annul each other, but each attracts its own type of event. Very frequently, however, the fortune or misfortune of the event is not indicated by the harmony or discord of the aspect, but is powerfully influenced by the dominant progressed aspect at the time acting as a Rallying Force.

The indicated major event may be expected during the time the progressed aspect is within approximately one degree of the perfect aspect. The same orb of influence is effective for sub-major-progressed aspects (major-progressed aspects of the Moon), for minor-progressed aspects, and for transit aspects. For an event to be attracted by any of the three types of progression it is not necessary that any other type of progression contribute to it. But during the period a major-progressed aspect is within the indicated distance from perfect there will occur several brief periods when due to the major-progressed Moon, or a minor-progressed planet, or both, or several minor-progressed aspects, forming an aspect with one of the planets involved in the major-progressed aspect, or affecting the house ruling the anticipated event, the thought cells working for the event are given unusual accessory energy. And it may confidently be expected the event will occur on one of these peaks of thought-cell activity.

The event indicated by a major-progressed aspect is not much influenced as to its fortune or misfortune by the harmony or discord of the sub-major aspect or minor-progressed aspect which gives its thought cells accessory energy. Within the larger pattern of conditions indicated by the major-progressed aspects, each sub-major aspect tends to work out in terms of a sub-major event or condition, and each important minor-progressed aspect tends to work out in terms of a minor event or condition.

Astrology does not foreshow events which are inevitable. It maps thought-cell activities which influence the thoughts and behavior and exert extraphysical power on the environment in such a way as to make certain events probable. The effort should be, through elimination, to reduce the probable events, and the periods when one or more of them will happen, to as few alternatives as possible. A good way to do this is in the following manner:

1. Eliminate all events which do not bear the characteristics of one of the two planets involved and all events not belonging to the houses influenced.

    SUN: Any progressed aspect of the Sun affects the vitality, the significance, and the authority.

    MOON: Any progressed aspect of the Moon affects the mental attitude, the domestic life, and the everyday affairs.

    MERCURY: Any progressed aspect of Mercury affects the mental interests, the facility or accuracy of expression, and increases the cerebral activity.

    VENUS: Any progressed aspect of Venus affects the emotions, the social relations, and the artistic appreciation.

    MARS: Any progressed aspect of Mars brings strife, haste, and increased expenditure of energy.

    JUPITER: Any progressed aspect of Jupiter affects the individual through abundance, increased optimism, and joviality.

SATURN: Any progressed aspect of Saturn brings work, responsibility, and economy or loss.

URANUS: Any progressed aspect of Uranus affects through something sudden, through a human agency, and brings change into the life.

NEPTUNE: Any progressed aspect of Neptune increases the imagination, increases the sensitivity, and attracts schemes.

PLUTO: Any progressed aspect of Pluto affects through groups, through subtle force, and brings coercion or cooperation.

2. Eliminate all events improbable because of lack of proper birth-chart planetary power, or lack of proper birth-chart aspects, or lack of proper birth-chart house activity.

3. Eliminate all events which the education and training of the individual, and the habit systems his thought cells have acquired make unlikely.

4. Eliminate from the remaining events those which do not fit into the pattern as influenced by Rallying Forces.

5. Eliminate from the few events that still remain those which the age of the individual make unlikely and which the environmental factors belonging to the two planets involved are not present to bring about.

Even after this process of elimination, there may remain several alternate events any one of which apparently might happen. But from the viewpoint that ascertaining the most probable event is not to foretell the inevitable future, but to be able to influence what actually happens, the residue thus found should be highly satisfactory; for one should not be unwilling to take steps facilitating several different events or deflecting several other different events, if by that effort the event when it actually occurs is made far more fortunate.

Chapter 2

Major Progressions of Sun and Angles

Serial Lesson Number 111
Original Copyright, 1934
Elbert Benjamine
a.k.a. C. C. Zain

Copyright 2014, The Church of Light

Correcting Ascendant for Latitude of Birth

Find (a) the difference in °s and 's between the house cusp for the nearest latitude to that of birth and the house cusp for the next nearest latitude to that of birth given in the table of houses.

Find (c) the difference in °s and 's between the nearest and the next nearest latitude to that of birth given in the table. In Dalton's, AP, AA, and RC tables this is always 1° (60')

Find (d) the difference in °s and 's between the true latitude of birth and the nearest latitude given in the table.

By proportion, reduce each term to 's, then multiply (a) by (d) and divide the product by (c). This gives (b), the correction for latitude.

By logarithms, from log. (d) subtract log. (c), and to the difference so found add log. (a). The result is the log. of (b), the correction for latitude. In using Dalton's, AP, AA, and RC tables log. (c) is always 1.3802.

When the true latitude of birth is less than the nearest latitude given in the table: If the table shows the 's decreasing with latitude, the correction is added. If the table shows the 's increasing with latitude, the correction is subtracted.

When the true latitude of birth is greater than the nearest latitude given in the table: If the table shows the 's decreasing with latitude, the correction is subtracted. If the table shows the 's increasing with latitude, the correction is added

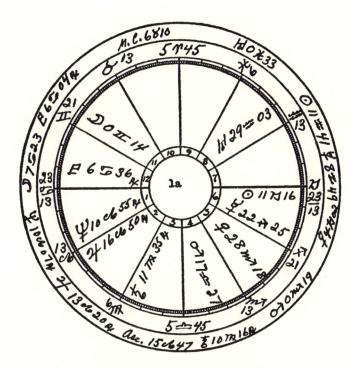

Majors: Birth Chart 1a

Jan. 2, 1920, 5:32 p.m. EST. 74W. 40:43N.

Major progressions in outer circle for Nov. 24, 1949.

Asc. semisquare Saturn r, June 25, 1924

Sun sesquisquare Saturn r, January 15, 1935

M.C. opposition Mars p, August 4, 1940.

Mercury conjunction Sun p, November 27, 1953.

M. C. conjunction Moon r, September 18, 1973.

Asc. sextile Mars p, July 7, 1977.

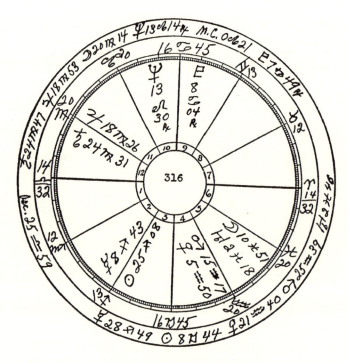

Majors: Birth Chart 316

Dec. 17, 1920, 1:30 a.m. MST. 105W. 39 45N

Major progressions in outer circle for April 24, 1934.

Sun sesquisquare Neptune r, April 5, 1924.

Asc. semisextile Jupiter r, June 19, 1925.

M.C. sextile Saturn r, August 6, 1928.

Asc. trine Mars p, August 9, 1929.

Mercury inconjunct M.C. p, March 2, 1937.

Mercury conjunction Sun p, May 23, 1951.

Chapter 2

Major Progressions of Sun and Angles

IT was Einstein's Special Theory of Relativity, ollowed to its practical and logical conclusions which led to the discovery of releasing and utilizing atomic energy. And it is this same Special Theory of Relativity followed to its practical and logical conclusions which indicates both how inner-plane energies operate and what can be done to cause them to work more to the individual's advantage.

As university scientists have conclusively demonstrated that time, distance and gravitation on the inner plane have properties radically different than they have on earth, should we expect inner-plane weather to operate according to the same laws weather operates on earth? Einstein's Special Theory of Relativity carried to its logical conclusions indicates that inner-plane weather affects the individual not merely according to his inner-plane constitution, but through certain time-space relationships that bring structural changes within his astral body.

Astrological energies constitute the inner-plane weather. How this inner-plane weather affects an individual, however, is not dependent upon any theory; for even as the time, distance and gravitation properties of the inner plane have been determined experimentally by university scientists, so have the properties of inner-plane weather, and how it works to affect individuals, groups, cities, nations and world affairs been determined experimentally, and through statistical studies carried out in the process of astrological research.

One of the outstanding influences of inner-plane weather is that when a person, creature or important event is born, it is born at a time when the inner-plane weather tends to coincide with the inner-plane makeup of that which is then born. Thus does the inner-plane weather at the time of his birth, as mapped by his birth chart, indicate the predisposition of an individual to develop abilities of a certain type. The planetary positions and aspects, whatever they may be, which indicate such a predisposition arc called its Birth-Chart Constants. The statistically ascertained Birth-Chart Constants of 30 different vocations arc set forth in the reference book *How to Select a Vocation*[1].

---

[1] Out of print. See *Astrology: 30 Years Research* by Doris Chase Doane.

The predispositions indicated by the inner-plane weather conditions at birth never manifest as events or diseases except during those periods when the appropriate thought cells receive commensurate additional energy from inner-plane weather mapped by progressed aspects.

Inner-plane weather consists of astrological vibrations in their infinite variety of combinations. Those mapped by progressed aspects enable planetary vibrations to reach and make active certain groups of thought cells. These thought cells have desires such as were imparted to them when they were formed and as indicated by the aspects of the planets mapping them in the birth chart. Such desires are temporarily altered by the planetary energy reaching them through the inner-plane weather mapped by a progressed aspect. And the additional energy thus reaching the thought cells not only gives them the power to influence the individual's thoughts and behavior, but it also gives them the psychokinetic activity that enables them to attract events of the kind they desire into his life.

By far the most important inner-plane weather is mapped by major-progressed aspects. Church of Light statistical research covering the lives of many thousands of persons indicates that every important event of life takes place during the period while a major-progressed aspect is present involving planets characteristic of the nature of the event, and which rule the birth-chart house governing the department of life affected. If more than one department of life is pronouncedly affected by the event, at the time it occurs there are always major-progressed aspects involving the ruler of each house governing these various departments of life.

The periods in his life when the individual is likely to experience a specific event, condition or disease toward which he has a predisposition are indicated by certain major-progressed aspects. These progressed aspects mapping inner-plane weather conditions which have been found always to coincide with the given event, condition or disease are called its Progressed Constants. The statistically ascertained Progressed Constants of 20 different events are set forth in the reference book *When and What Events Will Happen*[2], and both Birth-Chart Constants and the Progressed Constants of 160 different diseases are set forth in Course 16, *Stellar Healing,*

Both the birth-chart position and the progressed position of a planet act as terminals for the reception of planetary energy. Each terminal actually involved in the progressed aspect receives the energy of the progressed aspect in full volume. But unless the progressed aspect is from a major-progressed planet to its birth-chart place—in which case there are only two terminals—each

---

[2] Out of print. See *Astrology: 30 Years Research* by Doris Chase Doane.

progressed aspect has two other terminals not directly involved in the progressed aspect. Each of these two terminals not directly involved in the progressed aspect receives, through the principle of resonance, one-half as much energy as is received by each terminal directly involved.

It is important to understand that commonly a major-progressed aspect has four terminals because our research has determined that each Major-Progressed Constant of an event or disease is always reinforced by a minor-progressed aspect heavier than from the Moon to one of its four terminals at the time the event occurs or the disease develops; and that each reinforced Major-Progressed Constant of an event or disease is always released by a transit aspect heavier than from the Moon to one of its four terminals at the time the event occurs or the disease develops. And an independent minor-progressed aspect is always released by a transit aspect to one of the birth-chart or major-progressed terminals influenced by the minor-progressed aspect at the time the event takes place.

Before an ephemeris of Pluto was available to permit its aspects to be included, there seemed to be indications that events influenced by progressed aspects of Sun or Mars occasionally took place while the aspect was as much as a degree and half from perfect. But as statistically indicated in C. of L. Astrological Report No. 61, published in the January, 1948, number of *The Rising Star*, in these instances while sometimes the zodiacal aspect was well over the one degree limit, at the same time there was a progressed parallel aspect involving the significant planet which was not over the one degree limit.

The more closely the planets approach the perfect progressed aspect the greater the amount of energy the temporary stellar aerial in the astral body is capable of picking up, radio fashion, and transmitting to the thought cells at its direct and indirect terminals, and the more capable these become of influencing events.

Due to the reinforcement effect of minor-progressed aspects to any of the four terminals of the major-progressed aspect, to the trigger effect of transit aspects to any of the four terminals of the major-progressed aspect, and to the physical environment through which events must come, the important events attracted by major-progressed aspects seldom arrive exactly on the date the progressed aspect is perfect. But other things being equal, they are more apt to arrive close to the date the major-progressed aspect is perfect than while the aspect is farther removed. Therefore, that the time and nature of the important events which will be attracted into the life—unless they are forestalled by precautionary actions—may be estimated in advance, it is essential that the time be known when each major-progressed aspect becomes perfect.

As major progressions arc measured by the ratio of the movements of the planets during one apparent solar day releasing energy which causes the chief structural changes within the astral body that takes place during one astrological year of life, the movements and positions of the planets each four minutes after birth indicate the structural changes that take place within the astral body each corresponding day after birth; the movements and positions of the planets each two hours after birth spread the structural changes so shown over each corresponding month of life after birth; and the movements and the positions of the planets each day after birth indicate the structural changes and events attracted during the corresponding year and time of year of life.

The noon positions (or midnight positions if a midnight ephemeris is used) of the planets as given in the ephemeris must thus represent their major-progressed positions for some year, month and day of calendar time either before or after birth. And as on an average the progressed positions of the planets on the birthday are no closer or farther from making perfect progressed aspects than the progressed positions of the planets for any other day of the year, the calendar date which corresponds to the ephemeris positions of the planets on the day of birth is the most convenient starting point for calculating the calendar date any major-progressed aspect is perfect. Its originator called the calendar date thus found the LIMITING DATE.

Finding the Limiting Date

The Limiting Date (abbreviated L.D.) is the date in calendar time corresponding to the major-progressed positions of the planets on the day of birth as they are shown in the ephemeris. Convert the EGMT Interval of birth into months and days of calendar time by dividing the hours by 2 and calling the result months, and dividing the minutes by 4 and calling the result days.

If the EGMT Interval of birth is minus, add the calendar interval thus found to the year and month of birth. If the EGMT Interval of birth is plus, subtract the calendar interval thus found from the year, month and day of birth. The L.D. thus found is the calendar starting point from which all major-progressed aspects and positions are calculated. As the birth-chart positions of the planets are calculated for an EGMT Interval, the most convenient time for finding the L.D. is while the chart is being erected. However, should an EGMT Interval on the day preceding or following birth be used in finding the planets, places, this must not be employed in finding the L.D. Instead, the EGMT Interval on the day of birth must be ascertained; *for the L.D. must always be calculated from the EGMT Interval on the day of birth.* On B. of L. student blanks a space is designated on which to write the L.D. It may be in the year of birth, in the year previous to birth, or in the year following birth. In writing it down be sure to include not only the month and day of month, but also the year in which it falls.

Example 1: Chart la, Jan. 2, 1920, has an EGMT Interval of plus 10h 32m What is the Limiting Date?

MAJOR PROGRESSIONS OF SUN AND ANGLES 29

10 divided by 2 gives 5 as the month. 32 divided by 4 gives 8 as the days. As the interval is plus, the 5 months, 8 days must be subtracted from Jan. 2, 1920. This gives July 24, 1919, as the L.D. This means that the places of the planets given in the ephemeris for Jan. 3, 1920 (one day after birth) are their major-progressed positions for July 24, 1920. The Map. D. for calendar year 1920 is thus Jan. 3, 1920.

Example 2: Chart 316, Dec. 17, 1920, has an EGMT Interval of minus 3h 30m. What is the Limiting Date?

3 divided by 2 gives 1 month with a remainder of 60 minutes. 60m plus 30m gives 90m. 90 divided by 4 gives 22½ as the days. As the interval is minus, this 1 month, 22½ days must be added to Dec. 17, 1920. This gives Feb. 9, 1921, as the L.D. This means that the positions of the planets on the day of birth, Dec. 17, 1920, are their major-progressed positions for Feb. 9, 1921; and that their positions as shown in the ephemeris for Dec. 18, 1920, are their major-progressed positions for Feb. 9, 1922. Likewise, the positions of the planets in the ephemeris for Dec. 28, 1920, are their major-progressed positions for Feb. 9, 1932. Which means that the Map. D. for 1932 is Dec. 28, 1920.

Example 3: The birth chart of Henry Ford chapter 5, (Serial Lesson 107), Course 10-1, *Delineating the Horoscope* has an EGMT Interval of plus 7h 56m. What is the Limiting Date?

7 divided by 2 gives 3 as the months, with a remainder of 60m. These added to 56m gives 116m 116 divided by 4 gives 29 as the days. As the Interval is plus, this 3mo 29d must be subtracted from July 30, 1863, which is the date of birth. This gives April 1, 1863, as the L.D. July 31, 1863, represents the major-progressed positions, and is the Map.D. for April 1, 1864; and Aug. 1, 1863, represents the major-progressed positions for April 1, 1865. and is thus the Map.D. for 1865.

Finding the Major Progression Date

Both the L.D. and the Major Progression Date should always be calculated from the date of birth in the ephemeris. Using the day preceding or following birth in the ephemeris is the most common source of error in calculating major progressions. The Major Progression Date (abbreviated Map.D.) is the ephemeris day which shows the major-progressed positions of the planets for the month and day of the Limiting Date, but for some calendar year. To find the Map.D. for any calendar year, count ahead in the ephemeris from the day of birth as many days as complete years have elapsed since the Limiting Date. The ephemeris day so located is the required Map.D. Examples 1, 2 and 3 illustrate the process.

Finding the Midheaven Constant

As explained in chapter 1 (Serial Lesson 19), the M.C. progresses—by major progression, by minor progression, and by transit progression—exactly the same number of signs, °s and 's that the Sun progresses through the zodiac during the same time. As the progressed aspects made by the M.C. and Asc. are extremely important—next in importance to those made by the Sun—it is advisable to reduce the work of calculating a series of them, once for all, in each chart by finding the Midheaven Constant.

The Midheaven Constant (abbreviated M.C.C.) is the distance in the chart of birth between the M.C. and the Sun in signs, °s and 's expressed as a plus or minus, so that when added to the sign °, and ' occupied by the M.C. the algebraic sum gives the sign, °, and ' occupied by the Sun. It is found by merely subtracting the smaller zodiacal longitude occupied by birth-chart M.C. or Sun, from the larger zodiacal longitude occupied by birth-chart M.C. or Sun, and placing before the signs, °s, and 's thus found the proper plus or minus sign.

Then, wherever the M.C. may be by progression—major, minor or transit—algebraically add the sign, °, and ' it occupies to the M.C.C. and the result is the sign, °, and ' occupied by the progressed Sun. And wherever the progressed Sun may be, change the sign before the M.C.C. and algebraically add it to the sign, °, and ' occupied by the progressed Sun and the result is the sign, °, and ' occupied by the progressed M.C.

Example 4: In chart 1a, the Sun is 11 Capricorn 16 and the M.C. is 5 Aries 45. From 10S 11° 16' subtract 1S 5° 45' and it gives 9S 5° 31'. As to find the position of the Sun the difference so found must be added to the M.C., the M.C.C. is plus 9S 5° 31'.

Example 5: In chart 316, the Sun is 25 Sagittarius 08 and the M.C. is 16 Cancer 45. From 9S 25° 08' subtract 4S 16° 45' and it gives 5S 8° 23'. As to find the position of the Sun the difference so found must be added to the M.C., the M.C.C. is plus 5S 8° 23'.

Example 7: In the Henry Ford chart chapter 5 (Serial Lesson 107), Course 10-1, *Delineating the Horoscope* the Sun is 7 Leo 06 and the M.C. is 12 Virgo 00. From 6S 12° 00' subtract 5S 7° 06' and it gives 1S 4° 54'. As to find the position of the Sun the difference so found must be subtracted from the M.C., the M.C.C. is minus 1S 4° 54'.

The Problems of Progressions

The calculations involved in chart erection, major progressions, minor progressions and transit progressions are chiefly the solution of problems in direct proportion such as are taught in grammar school. In each problem (a) : (b) :: (c) : (d).

In thus solving problems in proportion, as the product of the means is equal to the product of the extremes, when the two inner terms are given, multiply one by the other and divide the product by the outer term. When the two outer terms are given, multiply one by the other and divide the product by the inner term. The result is the answer.

Any of these problems in proportion can be solved in four different ways. They can be solved by direct proportion, they can be solved by logarithms, they can be solved with a slide rule, or they can be solved with The Church of Light Chart Calculator.

In mathematically handling proportions involving hours and minutes and °s and 's, the use of logarithms greatly reduces the labor. Each problem in proportion considered in this book can be worked either by direct proportion, or by logarithms. By either method the letter employed to designate each term of the proportion is as follows:

(a) is the ephemeris daily gain, or gain through some constant interval of time or space.

When only one planet or position is moving, as when a planet is moving to make an aspect with some birth-chart position, the ephemeris daily gain (a) is the daily motion of the planet. When both planets or positions are direct in motion, or when both planets or positions are retrograde in motion, subtract the ephemeris daily motion of the slower moving planet from the ephemeris daily motion of the faster moving planet. The result is (a) the ephemeris daily gain. When one planet or position is direct in motion and the other is retrograde in motion, add the two daily motions. Their sum is (a) the ephemeris daily gain.

(b) is the gain during some selected interval of time or space.

(c) is the constant interval of time or space.

(d) is some selected interval of time or space.

In employing direct proportion to solve problems in progression it is more convenient to work immediately with calendar time. But in employing logarithms it is more convenient to work the problem first in terms of progression time (EGMT Interval), and then convert the result so found into calendar time. Diurnal proportional logarithms such as are to be found in the back of most ephemerides are constructed to solve just such problems in proportion, term (c), which is always 1440 minutes (24 hours), being taken care of by the table.

The advantage of such logarithms, which are almost universally used in erecting birth charts to find how many °s and 's a planet moves during a given EGMT Interval, is that the logarithm of term (b) can be obtained merely by adding the logarithms of term (a) and (d); and the logarithm of term (d) can be obtained merely by subtracting the logarithm of term (a) from the logarithm of term (b).

To designate the birth-chart position of a planet it has become the custom to use the letter r after the planet, to designate a major-progressed planet to use the letter p after the planet, to designate a minor-progressed planet to use the letter m after the planet, and to designate a transit-progressed planet to use the letter t after the planet.

Finding the Major-Progressed Positions of the Planets on a Given Calendar Date

Find the plus or minus calendar interval in months and days the given date is from the nearest month and day of the L.D. Then find the Map. D. in the ephemeris for the L.D. from which the given calendar date is this number of months and days distant. Convert the calendar interval from the L.D. in that calendar year into EGMT Interval (major progression time) at the rate of each month being equivalent to 2 hours, and each day being equivalent to 4 minutes. If the calendar interval is plus the EGMT Interval thus found is plus; if the calendar interval is minus the EGMT Interval thus found is minus. Use this EGMT Interval on the Map. D. in the ephemeris exactly as if finding the birth-chart positions of the planets for this EGMT Interval on that ephemeris day.

Example 8: Find the major-progressed positions of the planets on Nov. 24, 1949, for chart 1a. In example 1 the L.D. is found to be July 24, 1919. Subtracting 7mo 24d from 11mo 24d gives a plus calendar interval of 4mo. Multiplying 4 by 2 gives a plus 8h EGMT Interval. Subtracting 1919 (L.D.) from 1949 gives 30. Adding 30 days to January 2, 1920 (date of birth) gives February 1 as the Map. D. Using the planetary positions on Feb. 1, 1920, and calculating their positions for a plus EGMT Interval of 8 hours, gives their major-progressed positions on November 24, 1949, as shown on page 23.

Example 9: Find the major-progressed positions of the planets on April 24, 1934, for chart 316. In example 2 the L.D. is found to be Feb. 9, 1921. Subtracting 2mo 9d from 4mo 24d gives a plus 2mo 15d calendar interval. Multiplying 2 by 2 gives 4h. Multiplying 15 by 4 gives 60m, or 1h. There is thus a plus 5h EGMT Interval. Subtracting 1921 (L.D.) from 1934, gives 13. Adding 13 days to Dec. 17, 1920 (date of birth) gives Dec. 30, 1920, as the Map. D. Using the planetary positions on Dec. 30, 1920, and calculating their positions for a plus EGMT Interval of 5h, gives their major-progressed positions on April 24, 1934, as shown on page 24.

Finding the Major, Minor or Transit-Progressed M.C. on a Given Date

First find the sign, °, and ' occupied by the progressed Sun on the given calendar date. Change the sign before the M.C.C. and algebraically add the M.C.C. to the sign, °, and ' occupied by the progressed Sun. The result is the precise progressed M.C.

Example 10: Find major-progressed M.C. for chart 1a on November 24, 1949. In example 4 the M.C.C. for this chart is shown to be plus 9S 5° 31 '. Major-progressed Sun on November 24, 1949, is 11 Aquarius 41. Subtracting 9S 5° 31' from 11S 11° 41' gives 2S 6° 10'. Thus progressed M.C. is 6 Taurus 10.

Example 11: Find major-progressed M.C. for chart 316 on April 24, 1934. In example 5 the M.C.C. of this chart is shown to be plus 5S 8° 23'. Major-progressed Sun on April 24, 1934, is 8 Capricorn 44. Subtracting 5S 8° 23' from 10S 8° 44' gives 5S 0° 21'. Thus progressed M.C. is 0 Leo 21.

Finding the Major, Minor or Transit-Progressed Asc. on a Given Date

In a table of houses look between the two columns within which the progressed M.C. occurs, and find (a) the °s and 's between the nearest and next nearest Asc. given for the latitude nearest that of birth.

Find (c) the °s and 's between the nearest and next nearest M.C. given in the table. In Dalton's, AP, Raphael's and RC tables this is always 1° (60').

Find (d) the °s and 's between the true M.C. and the M.C. given in the table.

By proportion reduce each term to 's, then multiply (a) by (d) and divide the product by (c). This gives (b), the distance the Asc. is from the nearest Asc. given in the table for the nearest latitude given in the table.

By logarithms, to log. (a) add log. (d), and from the sum so found subtract log. (c). The result is log. (b), the distance the Asc. is from the nearest Asc. given in the table for the nearest latitude given in the table.

If the true M.C. is smaller than the M.C. given in the table, subtract (b) from the nearest Asc. in the table. If the true M.C. is greater than the M.C. given in the table, add (b) to the nearest Asc. in the table.

This gives the Asc. for the latitude given in the table. If the latitude of birth is not precisely that given in the table, use the *Correction for Latitude* given on page 22.

Example 12: Find major-progressed Asc. for chart 1a on November 24, 1949. In example 10 the major-progressed M.C. for this date is shown to be 6 Taurus 10. AP and Raphael's tables give the Asc. for 6 Taurus as 15 Leo 39 and the Asc. for 7 Taurus as 16 Leo 24. The difference (a) is thus 45'. As 6 Taurus 10 is 10' more than 6 Taurus, (d) is 10'. (c) is 60'. By proportion, multiplying 45 by 10 gives 450. 450 divided by 60 gives 7½'. By logarithms, the sum of log. (a) 1.5051 and log. (d) 2.1584 is 3.6635. Subtracting log. (c) 1.3802 from 3.6635 gives 2.2833, which is the log. of (b) 7½'. To the Asc. for 6 Taurus, which is 15 Leo 39, we add 8' (considering the ½ as 1), which, as the table is for the precise latitude of birth, gives the progressed Asc. as 15 Leo 47'.

Example 13: Find major-progressed Asc. for chart 316 on April 24, 1934. In example 11 the major-progressed M.C. for this date is shown to be 0 Leo 21. Dalton's table gives the Asc. for 0 Leo in latitude 40 as 25 Libra 38, and the Asc. for 1 Leo as 26 Libra 27. The difference (a) is 49'. As 0 Leo 21 is 21' more than 0 Leo, (d) is 21'. (c) is 60'. By proportion, multiplying 49 by 21 gives 1029. 1029 divided by 60 gives 17. By logarithms, the sum of log. (a) 1.4682 and log. (d) 1.8361 is 3.3043. Subtracting log. (c) 1.3802 from 3.3043 gives log. 1.9241, which is the log. of (b) 17'. To the Asc. for 0 Leo, which is 25 Libra 38, we add 17', which gives the progressed Asc. for the latitude given in the table as 25 Libra 55.

But as the true latitude of birth is 39° 45', there is a correction to be made for (d) the 15' difference in latitude. Under the 0 Leo column the table gives 25 Libra 52 for latitude 39, and 25 Libra 38 for latitude 40, a difference of (a) 14'. (c) is 60'. Following the instructions given on page 22, by proportion, multiplying(a) 14 by (d) 15 gives 210. Dividing 210 by 60 gives (b) 3½'. By logarithms, subtracting log. (c) 1.3802 from log. (d) 1.9823 gives .6021. Adding log. (a) 2.0122 to .6021 gives 2.6143, which is the log. of (b) 3½'.

As the true latitude is less than the nearest latitude given in the table and the 's are decreasing with latitude, we add the correction of 3½' to 25 Libra 55, which (considering the ½ as 1) gives the progressed Asc. as 25 Libra 59.

Finding the Calendar Date on Which a Major Progressed Aspect Between Planets is Perfect

Find the Map. D. in the ephemeris nearest the ephemeris time the aspect is perfect.

Find (a) the daily gain in °s and 's of the one planet on the other as indicated on the Map. D. in the ephemeris.

Find (b) the °s and 's the aspect is from perfect.

In employing proportion (c) is 12 months or 365 days. In employing logarithms (c) is 24h EGMT Interval.

In employing proportion (d) is months and days of calendar time from the L.D. in the calendar year it takes the planets to close the gap (b) and make the perfect aspect.

In employing logarithms (d) is the number of hours and minutes of EGMT Interval on the Map.D. it takes the planets to close the gap (b) and make the perfect aspect. This EGMT Interval must then be converted into its equivalent plus or minus calendar interval at the rate of each 2 hours being equal to 1 month and each 4 minutes equal to 1 day. By either method if the aspect is formed before the positions given in the ephemeris, subtract the calendar interval thus found from the L.D. in the calendar year. If the aspect is formed after the positions given in the ephemeris, add the calendar interval thus found to the L.D. in the calendar year. This gives the calendar date the aspect is perfect.

By proportion, to find (d) multiply (b) by (c) and divide by (a).

By logarithms, to find (d) subtract log. (a) from log.(b).

Example 14: The L.D. for chart 1a was found to be July 24, 1919. On what date does the Sun make the conjunction with Uranus r by major progression?

Uranus r is 29 Aquarius 03. Turning to the 1920 ephemeris we find the Sun on Feb. 19, 1920, in 29 Aquarius 34, and thus (b) 31 ' past the perfect aspect. Between Feb. 18 and Feb. 19, 1920, the Sun is moving (a) 61'.

By proportion, multiplying (b) 31 by (c) 12 gives 372. Dividing 372 by (a) 61 gives the calendar interval (d) as 6 6/61 months, or 6mo 3d.

By logarithms, subtract log. (a) 61', 1.3730 from log. (b) 31', 1.6670, and it gives log. .2940, which is the log. of (d) 12h 12m. Dividing 12 by 2 gives 6mo. Dividing 12 by 4 gives 3 days.

Counting ahead in the ephemeris from the day of birth, January 2, 1920, we find that Feb. 19 is 48 days later. Adding 48 years to the L.D., July 24, 1919, gives 1967 as the calendar year for Map. D. Feb. 19, 1920. As the aspect was formed before the positions given in the ephemeris on Feb. 19, 1920, we subtract the calendar interval 6mo 3d from July 24, 1967. This gives the date of progressed Sun conjunction Uranus r as January 21, 1967.

Progressing the Sun

Examples of finding the dates of major-progressed aspects of the other planets will be found in chapters 3 and 4 (Serial Lessons 112 and 113). For precision the calendar date on which each progressed aspect involving the Sun is perfect should be determined in the manner above indicated. But as the daily motion of the Sun varies only from 57' to 61', its approximate major progression per month is 1/12 of this, or approximately 5'; and 1' progression is thus equivalent approximately to 6 days of calendar time. Thus when there is no need for precision it is more convenient to work progressed aspects of the Sun by proportion.

Example 6: Find date on which in chart 1a major-progressed Sun makes the semisquare with Venus r. Venus is 28 Scorpio 18. The Sun must therefore reach 13 Capricorn 18 to make the semisquare. In example 1, we found the L.D. for this chart to be July 24, 1919. On January 4, 1920, the ephemeris shows the Sun 12 Capricorn 51. It must therefore move 27' to make the aspect. Dividing 27 by 5 ('s of Sun travel per month) gives 5mo. Multiplying the remaining 2' by 6 (days the Sun travels in 1') gives us 12d.

Counting ahead in the ephemeris from the day of birth, January 2, 1920, we find January 4 is 2 days later. Adding 2 years to the L.D. July 24, 1919, gives 1921 as the calendar year for the Map. D. As the aspect was formed after the positions given in the ephemeris, we add the 5mo 12d to July 24, 1921, and it gives the date of Sun semisquare Venus r as January 6, 1922.

When the actual travel of the Sun on the Map. D., 61', is used, the more precise date obtained by either proportion or logarithms is January 3, 1922. The problem worked out in detail by logarithms is given on page 3 of chapter 1 (Serial Lesson 19).

Finding the Sign, °, and ' on the M.C. for a Given Asc.

If the table of houses does not give the precise latitude of birth, find the Correction for Latitude as explained on page 22.

When the true latitude is less than the nearest latitude given in the table: If the table shows the 's decreasing with latitude, the correction is subtracted. If the table shows the 's increasing with latitude, the correction is added.

When the true latitude of birth is greater than the nearest latitude given in the table: If the table shows the 's decreasing with latitude, the correction is added. If the table shows the 's increasing with latitude, the correction is subtracted.

This gives the Asc. for the nearest latitude given in the table.

Find (a) the °s and 's between the nearest and the next nearest M.C. in the table. In Dalton's, AP, Raphael's and RC tables this is always 1° (60').

Find (c) the °s and 's between the nearest and the next nearest Asc. given in the table.

Find (d) the °s and 's between the true Asc. corrected for the latitude given in the table, and the nearest Asc. for that latitude given in the table.

(b) is the distance the true M.C. is from the nearest M.C. given in the table.

By proportion, to find (b), multiply (a) by (d) and divide the product by (c). By logarithms, add log. (a) to log. (d) and from their sum subtract log. (c).

Example 15: In chart 1a what sign, ° and ' is on the M.C. when progressed Asc. makes the conjunction with Neptune r? To make the conjunction the progressed Asc. must move to 10 Leo 55. Looking in the table of houses for New York we find the nearest Asc. 11 Leo 08, with 30 Aries 00 on the M.C. The next nearest Asc. is 10 Leo 24. The difference (c) is 44'. The difference (d) between 10 Leo 55 and 11 Leo 08 is 13'. By proportion, multiplying (a) 60 by (d) 13 gives 780. Dividing 780 by (c) 44 gives 18'. By logarithms, adding log. (a) 1.3802 to log. (d) 2.0444 gives log. 3.4246. Subtracting log. (c) 1.5149 from 3.4246 gives 1.9097, which is the log. of (b) 18'.

As the Asc. when the aspect is complete is less than the nearest Asc. given in the tables, the 18' must be subtracted from 30 Aries 00. This gives the progressed M.C. 29 Aries 42.

Example 16: In chart 316 what sign, ° and ' is on the M.C. when progressed Asc. makes the trine with Pluto r? To make the trine with Pluto r the Asc. must move to 8 Scorpio 04. Dalton's table of houses shows 15 Leo 00 on the M.C. when 7 Scorpio 40 is on the Asc. in lat. 40, and 8 Scorpio 01 on the Asc. in lat. 39. As chart 316 is erected for lat. 39:45, there is a correction to be made for (d) 15' of latitude. (a) is 21', the difference between 7 Scorpio 40 and 8 Scorpio 01. Multiplying (a) 21' by (d) 15' gives 315. 315 divided by (c) 60' gives the correction for latitude as 5'. Subtracting this 5' from 8 Scorpio 04 shows that when 8 Scorpio 04 is on the Asc. in lat. 39 :45, 7 Scorpio 59 is on the Asc. in lat. 40, the lat. given in the table. We need to find, therefore, the sign, °, and ' on the M.C. when the table shows 7 Scorpio 59 on the Asc. in lat. 40.

In lat. 40 the table shows 7 Scorpio 40 as the nearest Asc. and 8 Scorpio 27 as the next nearest. The difference (c) is 47'. The difference (d) between 7 Scorpio 40 and 7 Scorpio 59 is 19'. By proportion, multiplying (a) 60 by (d) 19 gives 1140. Dividing 1140 by (c) 47 gives 24'. By logarithms, adding log. (a) 1.3802 to log. (d) 1.8796 gives log. 3.2598. Subtracting log. (c) 1.4863 from 3.2598 gives 1.7735, which is the log. of (b) 24'.

As the Asc. when the aspect is complete is more than the nearest Asc. given in the table, the 24' must be added to 15 Leo 00. This gives the progressed M.C. 15 Leo 24.

Finding the Calendar Date from Major, Minor or Transit-Progressed M.C.

Algebraically add the sign, °, and ' of the progressed M.C. to the M.C.C. The result is the sign, °, and ' occupied by the progressed Sun on the sought calendar date. Thus when the sign, °, and ' occupied by the Asc. when it makes an aspect is determined, the sign, °, and ' on the M.C. for this Asc. can be ascertained as above explained. And when the sign, °, and ' occupied by the progressed M.C. when it makes an aspect is determined—as when it makes an aspect to a birth-chart planet—this can be used. In either case, from the M.C. find the sign, °, and ' occupied by the progressed Sun by algebraically adding to it the M.C.C. Then find the calendar date on which the progressed Sun occupies the sign, °, and ' so found. This is the precise date on which the progressed Asc. or M.C. makes the aspect, or reaches the given sign, °, and ' of the zodiac.

Example 17: In chart 1a, on what date does major-progressed Asc. make the conjunction with Neptune r? In example 15 we found the aspect is perfect when 29 Aries 42 is on the progressed M.C. In example 4 we found the M.C.C. for this chart to be plus 9S 5° 31'. Adding 9S 5° 31' to 1S 29° 42' gives the major-progressed position of the Sun 11S 5° 13'. On January 26, 1920, the ephemeris gives the Sun 5 Aquarius 15. This is 2' past the required position, and as the Sun moves at the rate of 1' for each 6 days by major progression, this is equivalent to 12 days to be subtracted from the L.D. July 24, in the calendar year, giving July 12. As January 26 is 24 days after birth, we add 24 years to the year of the L.D., 1919. Asc. is conjunction Neptune r July 12, 1943.

Example 18: In chart 316, on what date does major-progressed Asc. make the trine with Pluto r? In example 16 we found the aspect is perfect when 15 Leo 24 is on the M.C. In example 5 we found the M.C.C. for this chart to be 5S 8° 23'. Adding 5S 8° 23' to 5S 15° 24' gives the major-progressed position of the Sun as 10S 23° 47'. On January 14, 1921, the ephemeris gives the Sun 23 Capricorn 49. This is 2' past the required position, and as the Sun moves at the rate of 1' for each 6 days major progression, this is equivalent to 12 days to be subtracted from the L.D. February 9, in the calendar year, giving (ignoring the 31 days in January) January 27. As January 14 is 28 days after birth, we add the 28 years to the year of the L.D., 1921. Asc. is trine Pluto r January 27, 1949.

Finding the Progressed Zodiacal Motion of Major, Minor or Transit M.C. or Asc.

In a table of houses find the nearest Asc. to that the motion of which is to be ascertained for the latitude nearest that of birth. The difference in Asc. motions between consecutive latitudes is so small that using the motion for the nearest latitude is sufficiently precise.

Find (a) the difference in °s and 's between the nearest and the next nearest Asc. given in the two columns within which the progressed Asc. is found.

Find (c) the difference in °s and 's between the nearest and the next nearest M.C. given in the same two columns in the table. In Dalton's, AP, Raphael's and RC tables this is always 1° (60').

Find (d) the daily motion of the Sun in °s and 's as given in the ephemeris on the Map. D., MED, or Transit Date. This is also the number of °s and 's traveled by the progressed M.C. during the same progressed interval. It is the daily motion of the M. C. on the Map. D., MED, or Transit Date.

By proportion, multiply (a) by (d) and divide the product by (c). This gives (b). By logarithm, add log. (a) to log. (d), and from the sum subtract log. (c). This gives log. (b). (b) thus found is the °s and 's the Asc. moves during the same major, minor or transit progression interval moved by the Sun. It is the daily motion of the Asc. on the Map. D. MED, or Transit Date.

Finding the Calendar Date on Which an Aspect Involving Major-Progressed M.C. or Asc. is Perfect

From the daily motion of the M.C. or Asc. on the Map. D., and the daily motion of the planet on the Map. D., find (a) the gain of the one on the other in °s and 's. If the aspect is from progressed M.C. or Asc. to a birth-chart position, (a) is the daily motion of M.C. or Asc.

Find (b) the °s and 's the aspect is from perfect. To find (b) first find the sign, °, and ' occupied by the progressed M.C. or Asc. on the Map. D. Then find the sign, °, and ' occupied by the progressed planet on the Map. D. The °s and 's which are less subtracted from the °s and 's which are greater, gives the °s and 's the aspect is from perfect.

(c) is 12mo calendar time or 24h EGMT Interval.

With (a), (b) and (c) thus ascertained the date the aspect is perfect is found exactly as in finding the date on which a major-progressed aspect between planets is perfect.

Example 19: In chart 1a, on what date does major-progressed Sun make the opposition of progressed Asc.? On Feb. 20, 1920, the ephemeris shows Sun 0 Pisces 34. Subtracting the M.C.C. 9S 5° 31' found in example 4, from 12S 0° 34' gives the progressed M.C. for this Map. D. 25 Taurus 03. The Asc. when 25 Taurus 03 is on the M.C. as worked from the table of houses for New York is 0 Virgo 31. Progressed Sun, moving faster than progressed Asc. is thus (b) 3' past the perfect opposition. The Sun on Feb. 20, and therefore the M.C., is moving 60'. The Asc. is moving 48' while the M.C. moves 60'. The gain (a) of the Sun on the Asc. is the difference between 48' and 60' or 12'.

By proportion, multiplying (b) 3 by (c) 12 gives 36. Dividing 36 by (a) 12 gives 3mo. By logarithms, subtracting log. (a) 2.0792 from log. (b) 2.6812 gives log. (d) .6020 which is the log. of 6h. Dividing 6 by 2 gives 3mo. Subtracting the 3mo from the L.D. July 24, in the calendar year, gives April 24. Feb. 20 is 49 days after the day of birth on Jan. 2. To the year of the L.D., 1919, we therefore add 49 years. Progressed Sun is opposition Asc. *p* April 24, 1968.

Example 20: In chart 316, when does major-progressed Mercury make the sextile with major-progressed Asc.? The Map. D. for 1930 is 9 days after birth, or Dec. 26, 1920. The ephemeris position of Mercury on this date is 22 Sagittarius 23. The position of the Sun on Dec. 26, 1920, is 4 Capricorn 27. In example 5 we found the M.C.C. of this chart to be plus 5S 8° 23'. Subtracting 5S 8° 23' from 10S 4° 27' gives the progressed M.C. on the Map. D. 26 Cancer 04. Dalton's table of houses shows 22 Libra 19 on Asc. in lat. 40 when 26 Cancer 00 is on M.C. Asc. moves 50' while M.C. moves 60'. Thus when 26 Cancer 04 is on the M.C. 22 Libra 22 is on the Asc. in lat. 40. As explained in example 13 there is a further correction of 3' to be added which gives the Asc. in lat. 39 :45 as 22 Libra 25.

As the Asc. on Map. D. is 22 Libra 25, and Mercury is 22 Sagittarius 23, the distance aspect is from perfect (b) is 2'.

The Sun on Dec. 26, and therefore the M.C., is moving 61'. To find how far Asc. moves while M.C. moves 61', as previously explained, multiply (a) 50 by (d) 61. This gives 3050. Then divide by (c) 60, which gives the daily motion of the Asc. (b) as 51'. The daily motion of Mercury on Jan. 26, 1920, is 1° 31'. The daily gain is thus 40'.

By proportion, multiplying (b) 2 by (c) 12 gives 24. Dividing 24 by (a) 40 gives (d) 24/40mo or 18d. By logarithms, subtracting log. (a) 1.5563 from log. (b) 2.8573 gives 1.3010 which is log. (d) 1h 12m. Dividing this 72m by 4 gives 18d. As Mercury is moving faster than the Asc. the aspect is formed after the Map. D. Therefore the 18d must be added to Feb. 9, 1930. Progressed Mercury is sextile Asc. *p*, Feb. 27, 1930.

Chapter 3

Major Progressions of the Moon

Serial Lesson Number 112
Original Copyright, 1934
Elbert Benjamine
a.k.a. C. C. Zain

Copyright 2014, The Church of Light

Finding the Declination of Major, Minor or Transit-Progressed M.C. or Asc. for Any Given Calendar Date

First find the sign, ° and ' of progressed M.C. or Asc. for the given calendar date. As any house cusp has the same declination as does the Sun when in the same sign, ° and ', then find the declination of the Sun when in the indicated sign, ° and '. This is the declination sought.

Major-progressed Asc. of chart No. 317 on Jan. 19, 1925, is 18 Sagittarius 29. Looking in the ephemeris for the Sun close to this place, on Dec. 10, 1920, we find it 18 Sagittarius 09, and on Dec. 11, 1920, we find it 19 Sagittarius 10, and thus moving daily (c) 61' by zodiacal longitude. The difference between 18 Sagittarius 09 and 18 Sagittarius 29 is (d) 20'. The Sun is increasing daily (a) 5' by declination. Multiplying (a) 5 by (d) 20 gives 100. Dividing 100 by (c) 61 gives (b) 2' to be added to the 22 S 55 declination of the Sun on Dec. 10, giving the declination of major-progressed Asc. on Jan. 19, 1925, as 22 S 57.

Major-progressed M.C. of chart No. 317 on Jan. 19, 1951, is 26 Libra 36. Looking in the ephemeris for the Sun close to this place, on Oct. 19, 1920, we find it 25 Libra 48, and on Oct. 20, 1920, we find it 26 Libra 48, and thus moving daily (c) 60' by zodiacal longitude. The difference between 26 Libra 48 and 26 Libra 36 is (d) 12'. The Sun is increasing daily (a) 22' by declination. Multiplying (a) 22 by (d) 12 gives 264. Dividing 264 by (c) 60 gives (b) 4' to be subtracted from the 10 S 20 declination of the Sun on Oct. 20, giving the declination of major-progressed M.C. on Jan. 19, 1951, as 10 S 16.

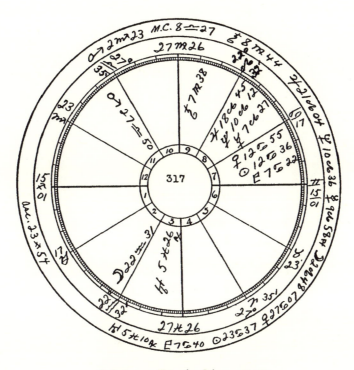

Majors: Birth Chart 317

July 4, 1920, 5:00 p.m. CST. 90W. 30N.
L.D. Jan. 19, 1920. M.C.C. minus 2S 14° 50'.

Major progressions in outer circle are for Jan. 19, 1932.

Feb. 17, 1925 Asc. parallel Venus *p*.

May 11, 1932 Moon conjunction Mercury *r*.

Sept. 29, 1933   Moon sextile Mars *r*.

July 11, 1934   Moon conjunction Saturn *p*.

Oct. 16, 1937   Moon trine Moon *r*.

May 10, 1938 Moon square Sun *p*.

Jan. 2, 1951   M.C. parallel Uranus *r*.

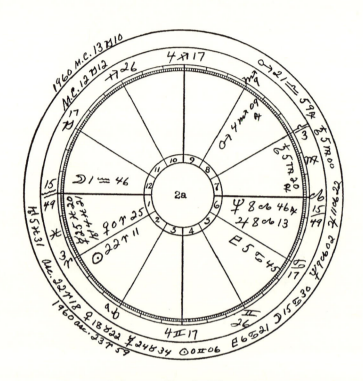

Majors: Birth Chart 2a

April 12, 1920, 3:00 a.m. MST. 108W. 40N.
L.D. May 12, 1920. M.C.C. minus 7S 12° 06'.

Major progressions in outer circle are for May 21, 1959.

M.C. 1959 is 22 S 53. M.C. 1960 is 22 S 48.
Asc. 1959 is 08 N 41. Asc. 1960 is 09 N 18.

Oct. 20, 1920   Moon opposition Jupiter r.

Nov. 7, 1922   Moon square M.C. r.

March 21, 1925   Moon conjunction Venus p.

April 29, 1926   Moon conjunction Sun r.

April 6, 1927   Moon sextile Pluto r.

March 26. 1929   Moon square Uranus p.

Chapter 3

Major Progressions of the Moon

THER than that a progressed planet carries with it only one-half the power (astrodynes) it had at birth, the influence is the same whether the planet under consideration is a birth-chart planet receiving the aspect of a progressed planet or is a progressed planet making an aspect to a birth-chart planet or to another progressed planet. Therefore, instead of repeating the phrase, "making an aspect to or receiving an aspect from," when a planet makes or receives an aspect, we merely say it is involved in the aspect.

Each planet maps, both in the birth chart and by progression, a particular type of inner-plane weather. This type of inner-plane weather influences the desires of the thought cells in a manner characteristic of the planet mapping it. Thus from each planet involved in a progressed aspect we may expect the thought cells to use whatever psychokinetic power they gain from the aspect to try to bring into the life conditions and events characteristic of the planet.

Aside from the type of inner-plane weather indicated by the planets involved in the aspect, each aspect indicates weather that is favorable or unfavorable, or that has a special trend, which is distinctive of the aspect mapping it. This distinctive trend is indicated by the keyword of the aspect as given in chapter 2 (Serial Lesson 87), Course 8, *Horary Astrology*.

The inner-plane weather indicated by a progressed aspect chiefly influences the thought cells mapped by the birth-chart houses containing the terminals of the progressed aspect and the houses of the birth chart ruled by the planets involved. As the thought cells mapped by a house relate to a definite department of life, the houses involved show the departments of life chiefly influenced by the progressed aspect.

Progressed Aspects Involving the Sun

Any progressed aspect involving the Sun affects the vitality, the significance, and the authority.

The thought cells in the astral form mapped or ruled by the Sun are chiefly composed of thought elements of the type which relate to the persistence and significance of the Individual.

They express as the Power Urges, map the most deep seated traits of character, are particularly important in giving power to exercise authority over others, as indicating the relations with men in general, and as being the rulers of the electrical energies which give vitality. They not only denote the ability to exercise power over others, but the ability to get the esteem and confidence of those who exercise such authority.

Power and energy are not the same thing. Energy must be effectively directed to become power. Ability to dominate conditions through persistently directed desire, or willpower, resides primarily in the Individuality, or Sun dynamic structure, of the astral body.

Progressed aspects involving the Sun are very important because the activity of the Power thought-cells so largely determines the Individual's power. They indicate his ability to get along with those in authority, and his own estimation of himself or the esteem in which others hold him. He only gets honors when there is a progressed aspect involving the Sun.

Progressed Aspects Involving the Moon

Any progressed aspect involving the Moon affects the mental attitude, the domestic life, and the everyday affairs.

The thought cells in the astral form mapped or ruled by the Moon are chiefly composed of thought elements of the type which relate to the unconscious mind and the domestic life.

They express as the Domestic Urges, map the most open and receptive avenues to the unconscious mind, are particularly important as affecting the moods, the domestic life, the relations with the common people, the relations with women in general, and as being the rulers of the magnetic energy which influences the strength of the physical constitution and therefore the health.

The major-progressed Moon moves through all twelve houses and makes all possible aspects to the other planets in 27.3 years. Because its thought cells are so open an avenue for energy, its passage through each house in turn, averaging less than two and a half years, tends to bring the things signified by the department of life ruled by the house it is in at the time to the fore.

In some manner the popularity is apt to be affected by aspects involving the Moon. As it relates to the Mentality, the temporary mood is indicated by the planet to which it makes a progressed aspect.

Progressed Aspects Involving Mercury

Any progressed aspect involving Mercury affects the mental interests, the facility or accuracy of expression, and increases the cerebral activity.

The thought cells in the astral form mapped or ruled by Mercury are chiefly composed of thought elements of the type which relate to perception and intellectual effort.

They express as the Intellectual Urges. Mercury is the messenger. The planet with which it is involved in a progressed aspect influences the trend of thinking; and the departments of life mapped by the houses occupied by Mercury and the other planet involved in the aspect tend to become subjects of thought. Thus an aspect with Venus turns the thoughts toward mirth, an aspect with Mars turns the thoughts toward strife, an aspect with Jupiter turns the thoughts toward optimism and expansion, and an aspect with Saturn turns the thoughts to serious matters, to caution and to security.

While discordant progressed aspects involving Mercury are operative there is a tendency to attract misfortune through errors, which may be those of the person experiencing the aspect, or of others with whom he is dealing. Clerical errors, mistakes in addressing letters, mistakes in making change, documents purposely or by error wrongly worded, and saying the wrong thing, are common difficulties that arise.

Harmonious progressed aspects involving Mercury, on the other hand, give facility in writing and talking, and comparative freedom from error. They also favor travel; although there must be a progressed aspect involving the ruler of the third house for a short journey, and a progressed aspect involving the ruler of the ninth house for a long journey.

Progressed Aspects Involving Venus

Any progressed aspect involving Venus affects the emotions, the social relations, and the artistic appreciation.

The thought cells in the astral form mapped or ruled by Venus are chiefly composed of thought elements of the type which relate to feeling.

They express through the Social Urges, and the things they attract come into the life through social relations. There may be an attraction to music, dancing, art or other common avenue by which the emotions are given expression; or the emotional nature may merely become more sensitive to such contacts as already have been established. Neither a love affair nor marriage can be expected unless the ruler of the fifth or the ruler of the seventh is involved in a major-progressed aspect; but a progressed aspect involving Venus has a definite influence upon such affectional matters as are present.

If Venus is involved in a discordant progressed aspect, not only will there be a tendency for misunderstandings to develop, but the individual inclines to be unusually sensitive to imaginary slights or opposition. If he can realize this and train himself to overlook discord he will fare much better.

When Venus is involved in a harmonious progressed aspect, affectional matters move forward smoothly, and the attitude tends to be buoyant and pleasure seeking, attracting many happy occasions and joyous expressions. Venus inner-plane weather influences about one-fourth of all the good fortune experienced by mankind.

Progressed Aspects Involving Mars

Any progressed aspect involving Mars brings strife, haste and increased expenditure of energy.

The thought cells in the astral form mapped or ruled by Mars are chiefly composed of thought elements of the type which relate to energy.

They express through the Aggressive Urges. Whether the psychokinetic energy attracts infection, accident or combat, is diverted into mental creation, healing and surgery, into mechanical work, or into the building of something depends on whether the thought cells given activity are discordant or harmonious. Only in so far as it can be controlled is Mars energy beneficial; and even under the most favorable aspects what is gained is at the expense of initiative and strife. One must fight for any advantage Mars brings.

Mars is a social planet, and while its aspects are effective conflicts with others tend to develop. The individual feels less submissive, and is more active and aggressive than usual. If the aspect is favorable, it gives him the ability to win his objective in spite of opposition. But if the aspect is unfavorable he suffers severely from the antagonism of others.

Mars is also the mechanical planet, and its progressed aspects affect the relations with machines, with sharp instruments, and the various agencies which may cause accidental injury. Machines give trouble under adverse aspects involving Mars, and surgical operations and accidents take place only while some major-progressed aspect involving Mars is present.

Haste is often a contributing factor to such accidents. Impulse and over-exertion are Mars tendencies, and fevers and infection are attracted only while there is a progressed aspect involving Mars. Mars inner-plane weather influences about one-fourth of all the trouble experienced by mankind. Under Mars inner-plane weather cultivate patience and take it easy.

Progressed Aspects Involving Jupiter

Any progressed aspect involving Jupiter affects the individual through abundance, increased optimism, and joviality.

The thought cells in the astral form mapped or ruled by Jupiter are chiefly composed of thought elements of the type which relate to good fellowship.

They express through the Religious Urges, and the things they attract into the life are not derived from work and hardship, but from good fellowship and patronage. Jupiter is the salesmanship planet, and the things attracted by its thought cells are derived chiefly from the benevolence and good will of others. They give an optimism which tends toward expansion, and they incline toward thoughts of religion and business. Jupiter is a business planet, and contacts with merchants, bankers, the clergy, lawyers and doctors are particularly affected by the activity of its thought cells.

The most fortunate of planets, its thought cells use their psychokinetic power to bring Abundance. Even such afflictions as they bring are due to an excess of something, such as excess of food, or excessive richness of food which injures the health, excessive expenditures which affects the finances, over expansion which affects the credit, or too great generosity, carelessness or extravagance. Jupiter inner-plane weather influences about one-half of all the good fortune experienced by mankind.

Progressed Aspects Involving Saturn

Any progressed aspect involving Saturn brings work, responsibility, and economy or loss.

The thought cells in the astral form mapped or ruled by Saturn are chiefly composed of thought elements of the type which relate to security.

They express through the Safety Urges, and the things they attract into the life are derived from responsibility, perseverance, plodding labor, system, organization, hardship or loss. If the aspect is harmonious the work done is productive of commensurate gain; but if discordant, there is inadequate recompense for labor expended.

Saturn is a business planet, but the method it follows is always restrictive, and thus the opposite of that employed by Jupiter. His gains are made through economy, system, order, shrewdness, and taking advantage of the necessity of other persons to buy at the lowest figure. In selling under progressed aspects involving Saturn the appeal must be made by means of presenting a bargain; and in buying a harmonious aspect involving Saturn is the best influence to attract a bargain.

The most unfortunate of planets, its thought cells use their psychokinetic power to bring Poverty. The afflictions they bring are due to a lack of something, such as inadequate diet affecting the health, death or sickness affecting the home, or loss affecting finances. Saturn inner-plane weather influences about one-half of all the troubles and losses experienced by mankind. Under Saturn inner-plane weather keep your chin up and cultivate cheerfulness.

Progressed Aspects Involving Uranus

Any progressed aspect involving Uranus affects through something sudden, through a human agency, and brings change into the life.

The thought cells in the astral form mapped or ruled by Uranus are chiefly composed of thought elements of the type which relate to originality.

They express through the Individualistic Urges, and the things they attract into the life come suddenly, through some human agency, and inaugurate a change which after they have passed in some manner leaves the life on a higher mental level. They tend to bring into the life new persons and new conditions, to take out of the life old associates and old conditions, and to bring new ideas which profoundly affect the life.

Uranus is the radical planet. He has a code of his own and is utterly indifferent to convention. Thus unconventional attachments or unconventional views flourish when his thought cells are active. More than any other thought cells they tend to the formation of sudden strong attachments and the breaking of them. Breaking one attachment often coincides with forming another. Yet an attachment formed under a progressed aspect involving Uranus is apt to last only while the aspect is within the one effective degree of perfect.

Uranus has particular rule over astrology and the occult sciences, although both Neptune and Pluto incline also to such studies. When the progressed aspect involving Uranus is a strong one it divides the life as if one chapter had been finished and an entirely new one commenced. And the instrument by which such changes are brought about, often as a bolt from a clear sky, is always human. The planet rules the sign of the Man, and such favors as it brings come through some person attracted by the activity of its thought cells, and the misfortunes it attracts are due to some person exercising an undue influence over the life, or through some person's carelessness.

New inventions, and gadgets requiring electricity such as automobiles and radio sets, tend to get out of order under discordant progressed aspects involving this planet. And a peculiar thing about any of the events attracted by its thought cells is that no matter how favorable they are there is also some small loss, and no matter how unfavorable they are, they are accompanied by some small gain.

Progressed Aspects Involving Neptune

Any progressed aspect involving Neptune increases the imagination, increases the sensitivity, and attracts schemes.

The thought cells in the astral form mapped or ruled by Neptune are chiefly composed of thought elements of the type which relate to idealism.

They express through the Utopian Urges, and the things they attract into the life come without much effort, for Neptune dislikes hard work. He inclines to negativeness, to great sensitiveness and to day dreams, rather than to positive action. He also is unconventional, but less obviously so than Uranus. His thought-cell activity inclines the mind to advanced views, and to interest in occultism, psychic matters and astrology. But to make an astrologer other thought cells must be active enough to overcome the reluctance of those mapped by Neptune to learn how to handle the necessary astrological arithmetic.

Harmonious progressed aspects involving Neptune lead to vacations, outings and unusually pleasant experiences. Often a feeling akin to ecstasy is present. But even its more favorable aspects have a peculiar separative quality upon affectional relationships. The separation is not abrupt, as are those occasioned by Uranus, but quite gradual. Often there is a voluntary renunciation. Yet romantic attachments also may be formed.

The unfavorable events attracted by Neptune's discordant thought-cell activity usually have to do with unrealizable ideals formed by the individual, or to deliberate promotion schemes fostered to take advantage of him by others. Confidence men are represented by heavy afflictions involving Neptune; and less heavy afflictions indicate well-meaning promotion schemes which fail. Relative to the health, Neptune progressed aspects are present in all cases of poisoning, and by depressing the secretion of adrenalin and cortin they facilitate infection.

Neptune tends to exaggerate, and that which approaches under its progressed aspects always seems larger than later it turns out to be, except in those rare cases in which the individual, without effort, receives some amazing benefit. The big sweepstake and lottery winnings are almost always under Neptune aspects. But by far the most of the time big benefits that are promised turn out to be small benefits when realized. Threatened calamities, that cause vast worry and fear, either fail to arrive or on arrival are of minor consequence.

Imagination is active under Neptune thought-cell activity, and projects and plans that are attracted under discordant aspects tend to fizzle. Even those started under better aspects yield far less than anticipated. Usually what is promised by Neptune should be discounted by about 90%.

Progressed Aspects Involving Pluto

Any progressed aspect involving Pluto affects through groups, through subtle force, and brings coercion or cooperation.

The thought cells in the astral form mapped or ruled by Pluto are chiefly composed of thought elements of the type which relate to cooperation. The events they attract are unique in their power to attract the individual to participation in group activity of some kind which is sure to meet opposition from some other group.

They express through the Universal Welfare Urges, and the things they attract into the life come through groups. The groups the Pluto thought cells use their psychokinetic power to bring into the life may have for purpose some selfish advantage over others, or to benefit humanity. On its better side Pluto gives the impulse to work for Universal Welfare. But on its adverse side it tends to gangdom and racketeers.

It thus behooves an individual when progressed aspects involving Pluto are powerful, to use discrimination in joining forces with others, either those on the physical plane or those of the inner world. Under discordant progressed aspects an individual may become involved with the criminal underworld, be the object of kidnapers or be used as a tool by invisible racketeers. Yet under more harmonious progressed aspects there may be opportunity to join hands with others in an effort that is important for universal good.

No less than Uranus and Neptune, Pluto tends to stimulate interest in occult pursuits; and particularly has the power to connect up with intelligences on the inner plane. Under its thought-cell activity the individual may have the opportunity and the desire to do some spiritual work.

As do progressed aspects involving Uranus or Neptune, progressed aspects involving Pluto increase the sensitiveness of the nervous system and tend toward psychic experiences. The individual becomes unusually sensitive to the thoughts of those on either plane.

Progressed Aspects Involving M.C.

Any progressed aspect involving the M.C. affects the honor, the business and the publicity.

The thought cells in the astral form mapped by the M.C. are chiefly those which act as amplifiers. Whether the birth-chart M.C. or the progressed M.C., their activity attracts into the life events which influence the public standing. The type of event thus influencing publicity is determined by the characteristics of the planet involved in the aspect, and the department of life thus influencing publicity is indicated by the houses this planet rules. The business or honor also affects the departments of life indicated by the houses this planet rules.

Progressed Aspects Involving Asc.

Any progressed aspect involving the Asc. affects the health, the personality, and the personal affairs.

The thought cells in the astral form mapped by the Asc. are chiefly those which act as a ground wire through which the astral energy of the personality reaches the outside world. Whether the birth-chart Asc. or the progressed Asc., their activity has much significance in matters of health and how the personality affects others who are brought directly into contact with it; and how the things or people indicated by the planet involved in the progressed aspect affect the health, the personality, and bring changes into the personal life.

The planet involved in the progressed aspect determines by its characteristics the manner in which the health and personality will be influenced, and the houses it rules indicate the departments of life thus affecting the personality, and affected by the personality.

Major-Progressed Aspects of Moon Attract Only Sub-Major Events

Because long observation indicates that on the average a progressed aspect made by the Moon attracts an event only 1/7 as important as that attracted by a similar progressed aspect made by one of the other eleven positions, it is customary to designate major-progressed aspects made by the Moon as sub-major-progressed aspects. Progressed aspects made by any of the other eleven positions to birth-chart Moon, however, are on the average as powerful to attract events as those made to other birth-chart planets.

Finding the Motion by Declination of Major, Minor or Transit-Progressed M.C. or Asc.

The M.C. and Asc. have the same motion by declination that the Sun has when in the same zodiacal sign, °, and ' and moving through the same number of °s and 's of zodiacal longitude.

Turn in an ephemeris to the date when the Sun is approximately the same sign, °, and ' of the zodiac occupied by the progressed M.C. or Asc.

Find (a) the daily motion in °s and 's of the Sun on that date by declination.

Find (c) the daily motion in °s and 's of the Sun on that date by zodiacal longitude.

Find (d) the °s and 's the M.C. or Asc. moves by zodiacal longitude on the Map. D., MED., or Transit Date, as explained on page 39 of chapter 2 (Serial Lesson 111).

By proportion, multiply (a) by (d) and divide the product by (c). This gives (b). By logarithms, add log. (a) to log. (d), and from the sum subtract log. (c). This gives log. (b). (b) thus found is the °s and 's the M.C. or Asc. moves by declination during the same major, minor or transit progression interval moved by the Sun. It is the daily motion by declination of the M.C. or Asc. on the Map. D., MED., or Transit Date.

Example 21: In chart 317, what is the motion by declination of major-progressed Asc. on the Map. D. for 1925? The Limiting Date for this chart is Jan. 20, 1920. The Map. D. for 1925 is July 9, 1920. The progressed Asc. for this Map. D. is 18 Sagittarius 29, calculated according to the rule given on page 33 of chapter 2 (Serial Lesson 111).

Looking in the ephemeris for the date when the Sun is near 18 Sagittarius 29, on Dec. 10, 1920, we find it 18 Sagittarius 09, with a declination of 22 S 55, and on Dec. 11, 1920, we find it 19 Sagittarius 10, with a declination of 23 S 00. The daily motion by declination is (a) 5'. The daily motion by zodiacal longitude is (c) 61'.

Now to find (d) we must make the calculation explained on page 39 of chapter 2 (Serial Lesson 111). In this problem we look at a table of houses for latitude 30 and find that the difference between the nearest and the next nearest Asc. to 18 Sagittarius 29 is (a) 48'. The difference in the same column between the nearest and the next nearest M.C. is (c) 60'. The Daily motion of the Sun on the Map. D. (July 9, 1920) is 57'. Multiplying (a) 48 by (d) 57 gives 2736. Dividing 2736 by (c) 60 gives (b) 46' as the distance the Asc. moves while the Sun moves its 57' on the Map. D. Thus 46' becomes (d) of the main problem.

By proportion, multiplying (a) 5 by (d) 46 gives 230. Dividing 230 by (c) 61 gives (b) 4'. By logarithms, adding log. (a) 2.4594 to log. (d) 1.4956 gives 3.9550. Subtracting log. (c) 1.3730 from 3.9550 gives 2.5820, which is log. of (b) 4'. 4' is thus the daily motion by declination of major-progressed Asc. on the Map. D. for 1925.

Example 22: In chart 317, what is the motion by declination of major-progressed M.C. on the Map. D. for 1951? The Limiting Date for this chart is Jan. 19, 1920. The Map. D. for 1951 is Aug. 4, 1920. The progressed

M.C. for this Map. D. is 26 Libra 36, calculated according to the rule given on page 33 of chapter 2 (Serial Lesson 111).

Looking for the date when the Sun is near 26 Libra 36, on Oct. 19, 1920, we find it 25 Libra 48, with a declination of 9 S 58, and on Oct. 20, 1920, we find it 26 Libra 48, with a declination of 10 S 20. The daily motion by declination is (a) 22'. The daily motion by zodiacal longitude is (c) 60'.

On the Map. D. (August 4, 1920) the daily motion of the Sun is 57'. As the M.C. moves at the same rate the Sun moves, the daily motion of the M.C. (d) is also 57'.

By proportion, multiplying (a) 22 by (d) 57 gives 1254. Dividing 1254 by (c) 60 gives (b) 21'. By logarithms, adding log. (a) 1.8159 to log. (d) 1.4025 gives 3.2184. Subtracting log. (c) 1.3802 from 3.2184 gives 1.8382, which is the log. of (b) 21'. 21' is thus the daily motion by declination of major-progressed M.C. on the Map. D. for 1951.

Finding the Calendar Date on Which a Parallel Aspect Involving Major-Progressed M.C. or Asc. is Perfect

Find the declination in °s and 's occupied by the progressed M.C. or Asc. on the Map. D. If the aspect is to a birth-chart planet, find its birth-chart declination; but if it involves a progressed planet find the ° and ' of declination occupied by the planet on the Map. D.

From the daily motion by declination of the M.C. or Asc. on the Map. D., and the daily motion of the planet by declination on the Map. D., find (a) the gain of the one on the other in °s and 's. If the aspect is from progressed M.C. or Asc. to a birth-chart position, (a) is the daily motion by declination of M.C. or Asc.

Find (b), the °s and 's the parallel aspect is from perfect on the Map. D.

Then work the problem exactly as if finding the calendar date on which a major-progressed aspect between planets is perfect, as explained on page 34 of chapter 2 (Serial Lesson 111).

Example 23: Find the date on which in chart 317 progressed Asc. makes the parallel with Venus p. On Map. D. for 1925 (ephemeris date July 9, 1920) Venus is declination 22 N 58. On page 42 we found that on this same Map. D. progressed Asc. is declination 22 S 57. The aspect is thus (b) 1' from perfect on the Map. D. The ephemeris on July 9, 1920, shows Venus decreasing declination at the rate of 9' per day. We found in example 21 that the daily motion of the Asc. by declination is 4'. As Venus is decreasing in declination and Asc. (as shown by Sun when in same zodiacal degree) is increasing in declination, we add 9' to 4' which gives the daily gain (a) as 13'.

By proportion, multiplying (b) 1 by (c) 12 gives 12. Dividing 12 by (a) 13 gives the calendar interval (d) as 12/13 months, or 28 days. By logarithms, subtract log. (a) 2.0444 from log. (b) 3.1584, and it gives 1.1140 which is the log. of (d) 1h 51m, or 111m. Dividing 111 by 4 gives 28 days.

Adding this 28 days to January 19, 1925 (for which July 9, 1920, is Map. D.), gives progressed Asc. parallel Venus p Feb. 17, 1925.

Example 24: Find the date on which in chart 317 progressed M.C. is parallel Uranus r. Uranus r has declination 10 S 15. On Map. D. for 1951 (Aug. 4, 1920) on page 42 we found progressed M.C. has declination 10 S 16. The difference is (b) 1'. In Example 22 we found the daily motion of the M.C. by declination on this Map D. to be (a) 21'.

By proportion, multiplying (b) 1 by (c) 12 gives 12. Dividing 12 by (a) 21 gives the calendar interval (d) as 12/21 months, or 17 days. By logarithms, subtracting log. (a) 1.8361 from log. (b) 3.1584 gives 1.3223 which is the log. of (b) 1h 9m, or 69 minutes. Dividing 69 by 4 gives 17 days.

As progressed M.C. has passed the aspect on the Map. D., we subtract the 17 days from January 19, 1951. Thus major-progressed M.C. is parallel Uranus r January 2, 1951.

Calculating Aspects Made by Major-Progressed Moon

In order that the type and harmony or discord of the important inner-plane weather may be known far enough in advance that proper precautionary actions may be taken, all major-progressed aspects other than those made by the Moon should be calculated and tabulated for a number of years ahead. And major-progressed aspects made by the Moon should be calculated and tabulated at least one year ahead so that adequate precautionary actions may be taken relative to the accessory energy they may add to the inner-plane weather indicated by major-progressed aspects of the other planets when progressed Moon makes an aspect to a terminal of one of these other major-progressed aspects.

To facilitate calculating the major-progressed aspects of the Moon for a period of one year, and not inadvertently overlooking some important aspect, in addition to the birth-chart positions, including all declinations, it is well to write on the chart both the sign, °, and ' and the declination of the major-progressed M.C. and major-progressed Asc. calculated for the two consecutive Map. D's between which the progressed Moon calculations are to be made. Each of these Map. D's represents the Limiting Date within a given

MAJOR PROGRESSIONS OF THE MOON

calendar year. The difference between the sign, °, and ' of the progressed M.C. or Asc. on one Map. D. and the next Map. D. represents its progressed zodiacal motion during the corresponding year, and the difference between the declination of the M.C. or Asc. on one Map. D. and the next Map. D. represents its progressed motion by declination during the corresponding year. The zodiacal motion and the motion by declination of each of the planets between the two successive Map. D's show their motion by progression during the corresponding year. And as the positions of the planets in the ephemeris on the Map. D. show their positions for the L.D. within the corresponding calendar year, the calculations should start with the Map. D. and the calendar date within the year indicated by the L.D.

In calculating the major-progressed aspects of the Moon for a year it facilitates the work to start with the L.D. within one calendar year and before making the calculations tabulating one after another in the succession in which they form, all the aspects made by the Moon up to the L.D. of the following calendar year. The aspects thus start with one Map. D. and end with the following Map. D., the daily motion of all the planets between these two Map. D's being their major progression during the given year. Because the Moon's daily motion is so great it is much easier to calculate its progressed aspects by logarithms than by proportion. However, both methods will here be illustrated.

We will start with calendar date May 12, 1959, using Chart 2a on page 44, which has the major-progressed positions around it for this date. The Map. D. (date in the ephemeris) is May 21, 1920. On May 21, 1920, the daily motion of the Moon is (a) 14° 36'. The log. of this, which will be used for all aspects of the Moon to birth-chart positions, is .2159. Dividing 14° 36' by 12 gives the motion of the Moon per month by major progression as 1° 13', or 73' in 30 days.

1. Moon paralled Neptune *p*: The Moon is decreasing in declination (a) 2° 51' per day. 1/12 of this is 14', the amount of progression per month. Neptune *p* has declination 18 N 00. The Moon has declination 18 N 01. The difference is (b) 1'. 1/14 of 30 days is 2 days.

    By logarithms, subtracting log. of 2° 51' (a) .9254 from log. (b) 3.1584 gives 2.2330, which is the log. of (d) 8m. Dividing 8 by 4 gives 2 days. Adding the 2 days found by either method to May 12, 1959, gives Moon parallel Neptune *p* May 14, 1959.

2. Moon inconjunct Asc. *r*: To reach this aspect the Moon must move (b) 19' to 15 Leo 49. 19/73 of 30 days is 8 days.

    By logarithms, subtracting log. of 14° 36' (a) .2159 from log. (b) 1.8796 gives 1.6637, which is the log of (d) 31m. Dividing 31 by 4 gives 8 days. Adding the 8 days found by either method to May 12, 1959, gives Moon inconjunct Asc. *r* May 20, 1959.

3. Moon sextile Venus *p*: To reach this aspect the Moon must close a gap of (b) 2° 52'. Subtracting the 1° 13' Venus moves from the 14° 36' the Moon moves gives the daily gain (a) 13° 23'. Dividing this by 12 gives the gain per month as 1° 07'. In 2 months the gain is 2° 14'. This leaves 38'. 1° 07' is 67'. 38/67 of 30 days is 17 days.

By logarithms, subtracting log. of 13° 23' (a) .2536 from log. of 2° 52' (b) .9228 gives .6692, which is the log. of (d) 5h 08m. Dividing 5 by 2 gives 2mo with 60m remainder. Adding this remainder to the 08m gives 68m. Dividing the 68m by 4 gives 17 days. Adding the 2 months 17 days found by either method to May 12, 1939, gives Moon sextile Venus *p* July 29, 1959.

4. Moon sesquisquare M.C. *r*: To reach this aspect the Moon must move (b) 3° 47' to 19 Leo 17. At 1° 13' per month this takes 3 months with 8' remainder. 8/73 of 30 days is 3 days.

By logarithms, subtracting log. of 14° 36' (a) .2159 from log. (b) .8023 gives .5864, which is the log. of (d) 6h 13m. Dividing the 6 by 2 gives 3mo. Dividing the 13 by 4 gives 3d. Adding the 3 months, 3 days found by either method to May 12, 1959, gives Moon sesquisquare M.C. *r* August 15, 1959.

5. Moon sesquisquare Uranus *r*: To reach this aspect the Moon must move (b) 3° 51'. In 3 months it moves 3° 39'. To move the additional 12' takes 12/73 of 30 days, or 5 days.

By logarithms, subtracting log. (a) .2159 from log. (b) .7947 gives .5788, which is the log. of (d) 6h 20m. Dividing 6 by 2 gives 3mo. Dividing 20 by 4 gives 5d. Adding the 3 months, 5 days found by either method to May 12, 1959, gives Moon sesquisquare Uranus *r* August 17, 1959.

6. Moon sesquisquare Saturn *p*: To reach this aspect the Moon must close a gap of (b) 4° 30'. Saturn moves 2' and the Moon moves 14° 36'. The difference is the daily gain (a) 14° 34'. Dividing this by 12 gives the gain per month as 1° 13', or 73'. In 4 months it moves 4° 52'. To move the 22' it has gone too far, takes 22/73 of 30 days or 9 days. To make the aspect thus takes 3 months, 21 days.

By logarithms, subtracting log. (a) .2168 from log. (b) .7270 gives .5102, which is the log. of (d) 7h 25m. Dividing the 7 by 2 gives 3mo with a remainder of 60m. Adding the 60m to the 25m gives 85m. Dividing 85 by 4 gives 21d. Adding the 3 months, 21 days found by either method to May 12, 1959, gives Moon sesquisquare Saturn *p* September 3, 1959.

7. Moon semisquare Saturn *r*: To reach this aspect Moon must move (b) 4° 50'. In 4 months the Moon moves 4° 52'. To move the 2' it has gone too far, takes 2/73 of 30 days, or 1 day. It thus makes the aspect in 3mo, 29d.

MAJOR PROGRESSIONS OF THE MOON

By logarithms, subtracting log. (a) .2159 from log. (b) .6960 gives .4801, which is the log. of (d) 7h 57m. Dividing the 7 by 2 gives 3mo, with 60 remainder. Adding the 60m to the 57m gives 117m. Dividing the 117 by 4 gives 29d. Adding the 3 months, 29 days found by either method to May 12, 1959, gives Moon sesquisquare Saturn r September 11, 1959.

8. Moon sesquisquare Uranus p: To reach this aspect the Moon must close a gap of (b) 5° 01'. Uranus moves 1' and the Moon moves 14° 36'. The difference is the daily gain (a) 14° 35'. Dividing this by 12 gives the gain per month as 1° 13', or 73'. In 4 months the Moon moves 4° 52'. To move the other 9' takes 9/73 of 30 days, or 4 days.

By logarithms, subtracting log. (a) .2164 from log. (b) .6798 gives .4634, which is the log. of (d) 8h 15m. Dividing the 8 by 2 gives 4 mo. Dividing the 15 by 4 gives 4d. Adding the 4 months, 4 days found by either method to May 12, 1959, gives Moon sesquisquare Uranus p September 16, 1959.

9. Moon square Mars p: To reach the aspect the Moon must close a gap of (b) 6° 29'. Mars is moving retrograde 9', and the Moon is moving 14° 36'. To find the daily gain we add the two motions which gives (a) 14° 45'. Dividing by 12 gives the gain per month as 1° 14', or 74'. In 5 months the gain is 6° 10'. This leaves 19'. 19/74 of 30 days gives 8d.

By logarithms, subtracting log. of 14° 45' (a) .2114 from log. (b) .5684 gives .3570, which is the log. of (d) 10h 33m. Dividing the 10 by 2 gives 5mo. Dividing the 33 by 4 gives 8d. Adding the 5 months, 8 days found by either method to May 12, 1959, gives Moon square Mars p October 20, 1959.

10. Moon square Sun r: To reach this aspect the Moon must move (b) 6° 41'. In 5 months the Moon moves 6° 05'. This leaves 36'. 36/73 of 30 days gives 15 days.

By logarithms, subtracting log. (a) .2159 from log. (b) .5552 gives .3393, which is the log. of (d) 10h 59m. Dividing the 10 by 2 gives 5mo. Dividing the 59 by 4 gives 15d. Adding the 5 months, 15 days found by either method to May 12, 1959, gives Moon square Sun r October 27, 1959.

11. Moon square Asc. p: To reach this aspect the Moon must close a gap of (b) 6° 48'. The Asc. is moving (see chart page 44) 1° 41' and the Moon is moving 14° 36'. The difference is (a) 12° 55'. Dividing this by 12 gives a gain of 1° 05' per month. In 6 months the gain would be 6° 30'. This leaves 18'. 1° 05' equal 65'. 18/65 of 30 days gives 8 days (not so precise as by logarithms, as the gain is a trifle less than 1° 05' per month).

By logarithms, subtracting log. (a) .2691 from log. (b) .5477 gives .2786, which is the log. of (d) 12h 38m. Dividing the 12 by 2 gives 6 mo. Dividing the 38 by 4 gives 9d. Adding the 6 months, 9 days so found to May 12, 1959, gives Moon square Asc. *p* November 21, 1959.

12. Moon parallel Venus *p*: To reach this aspect the Moon must close a gap of (b) 1° 42'. The Moon is decreasing 2° 51', and Venus is increasing 22'. To find the gain we add these two motions which gives (a) 3° 13'. Dividing 3° 13' by 12 gives a gain of 16 per month. The gain in 6 months is 1° 36'. This leaves 6'. 6/16 of 30 days gives 11 days (not so precise as by logarithms, as the gain is a trifle more than 16' per month).

    By logarithms, subtracting log. (a) .8728 from log. (b) 1.1498 gives .2770, which is the log. of (d) 12h 41m. Dividing the 12 by 2 gives 6mo. Dividing the 41 by 4 gives 10d. Adding the 6 months, 10 days thus found to May 12, 1959, gives Moon parallel Venus *p* November 22, 1959.

13. Moon parallel Asc. *r*: To reach this aspect the Moon must move by declination (b) 1° 55' (Asc *r* is 16 5 06). By declination the Moon moves (a) 2° 51'. Dividing this by 12 gives 14' per month. In 8 months the Moon moves 1° 52'. This leaves 3' 3/14 of 30 days gives 6 days (not as precise as by logarithms, as Moon moves a trifle more than 14' per day).

    By logarithms, subtracting log. (a) .9254 from log. (b) 1.0977 gives .1723, which is the log. of (d) 16h 08m. Dividing the 16 by 2 gives 8mo. Dividing the 8 by 4 gives 2d. Adding the 8 months, 2 days thus found to May 12, 1959, gives Moon parallel Asc. *r* January 14, 1960.

14. Moon trine Mercury *r*: To reach this aspect the Moon must move (b) 9° 50'. In 8 months the Moon moves 9° 44'. This leaves 6'. 6/73 of 30 days gives 2 days.

    By logarithms, subtracting log. (a) .2159 from log. (b) .3875 gives .1716 which is the log. of (d) 16h 10m. Dividing 16 by 2 gives 8mo. Dividing 10 by 4 gives 2d. Adding the 8 months, 2 days found by either method to May 12, 1959, gives Moon trine Mercury *r* January 14, 1960.

15. Moon sextile Mercury *p*: To reach this aspect the Moon must close a gap of (b) 9° 04'. Subtracting the motion of Mercury, 2° 09', from the motion of the Moon, 14° 36', gives the daily gain (a) 12° 27'. Dividing this by 12 gives the monthly gain of the Moon as 1° 02'. In 9 months the Moon thus gains 9° 18', which is 14' too much. 1° 02' are 62'. 14/62 of 30 days gives 7 days. 7 days subtracted from 9 months gives 8 months, 23 days (not as precise as by logarithms, as Moon gains a trifle more than 1° 02' per month).

    By logarithms, subtracting log. (a) .2850 from log. (b) .4228 gives .1378, which is the log. of (d) 17h 28m. Dividing 17 by 2 gives 8mo, with 60m remainder. Adding the 60m to the 28m gives 88m. Dividing the 88 by 4 gives 22d. Adding the 8 months, 22 days to May 12, 1959, gives Moon sextile Mercury *p* February 4, 1960.

☙

Chapter 4

Major Progressions of the Planets

Serial Lesson Number 113
Original Copyright, 1934
Elbert Benjamine
a.k.a. C. C. Zain

Copyright 2014, The Church of Light

Know Your Inner-Plane Weather in Advance

To have the knowledge on which to base proper precautionary actions, you should at all times have calculated and set down in chronological order all your major-progressed aspects for several years ahead. This record of when aspects will be perfect should be kept in a convenient place and consulted frequently.

Before each of these aspects comes within its one degree of effective orb you should also calculate and set down the precise date it thus comes within the one degree of perfect. At one degree from the perfect aspect the inner-plane weather thus indicated is one-half as powerful as when the aspect is perfect, it increases in power until the aspect is perfect, then decreases until the aspect is one degree past perfect, when it again has half its peak power. Either before or after it is one degree from perfect its influence is negligible. But during the whole period it is within one degree of perfect, precautionary actions should be taken.

During the period when each important major-progressed aspect is within the one degree of effective orb you should keep informed a month or two ahead, just when minor-progressed aspects forming to one of its four terminals will reinforce its power—they thus reinforce all the time they are within one degree of perfect—and make it more likely at that time to attract an event of the character of the major-progressed aspect. While such reinforcing energy is present, special precautionary actions should be taken.

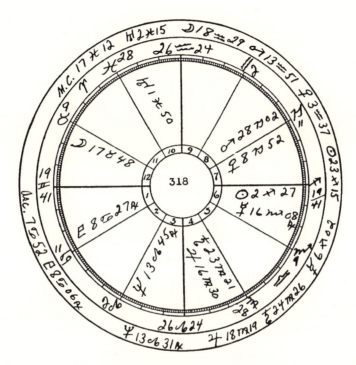

Majors: Birth Chart 318

November 24, 1920, 6:00 p.m. CST. 95W. 39N.
L.D. May 24, 1920. M.C.C. minus 2S 23° 57'.

Major progressions in outer circle are for May 24, 1941.

June 25, 1933	Venus trine Saturn p.
Sept. 29, 1936	Venus conjunction Mars r.
Nov. 27, 1937	Sun opposition Asc. r.
Aug. 29, 1938	Mercury square Uranus p.
Aug. 19, 1939	Venus sesquisquare Jupiter r.
Apr. 8, 1941	Mars opposition Neptune r.

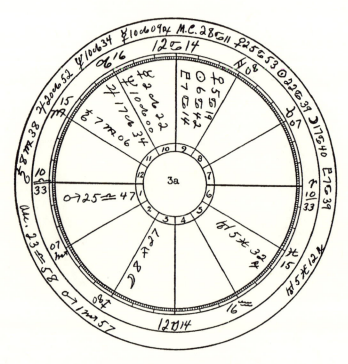

Majors: Birth Chart 3a

June 28, 1920, 12:23 p.m. CST. 89W. 40:40N.
L.D. March 22, 1920. M.C.C. minus OS 5° 32'.

Major progressions in outer circle are for March 22, 1937.

Jan. 1, 1924   Mercury inconjunct Uranus r.

Dec. 31, 1934   Sun sesquisquare Uranus r.

March 22, 1935   Saturn square Moon r.

Aug. 24, 1936   Sun semisquare Saturn r.

June 5, 1947   Venus trine Moon r.

Nov. 28, 1977   Mercury conjunction Jupiter r.

Chapter 4

Major Progressions of the Planets

ASIDE from the type of inner-plane weather indicated by the planets involved in a progressed aspect, each aspect indicates weather that tends to cause the thought cells it influences to use their psychokinetic power to influence the thoughts, behavior and the events that come into the life toward the distinctive trend indicated by the keyword of the aspect. The conjunction, parallel and inconjunct involving Venus or Jupiter are favorable, involving Mars or Saturn are unfavorable, and not involving one of these four planets, are neutral. The trine, sextile and semisextile between any two planets are favorable, but the opposition, square, semisquare and sesquisquare are unfavorable. The progressed aspect thus indicates positively whether the inner-plane energy is favorable or unfavorable.

But whether the thought cells thus influenced will use their psychokinetic power to bring fortunate or unfortunate events into the life depends upon how they feel. If through birth-chart harmony or discord, or through harmony or discord imparted to them since birth, they have been conditioned strongly enough to desire events and conditions that are favorable or unfavorable, the influence of the inner-plane weather mapped by a progressed aspect may not be powerful enough markedly to change this desire. And in that case the inner-plane weather may merely supply the energy to enable the thought cells to bring into the life an event which is of opposite fortune to that commonly indicated by the progressed aspect.

The thought cells of each planetary type can express characteristically through constructive thoughts and behavior or through destructive thoughts and behavior. To the extent their energy is channeled into their type of constructive thoughts and behavior does it decrease their power to influence their type of destructive thoughts and behavior. And as what happens to the individual often is markedly influenced by what he does, to the extent thoughts typical of the planet enter his mind and to the extent there are actions typical of the planet, under any progressed aspect involving the planet, whether harmonious, neutral or discordant, it is the part of wisdom to see to it they are typical of its constructive expression.

It is important to bear in mind that it is not the inner-plane weather mapped by an aspect which determines the fortune or misfortune of the event or condition coincident with it. Instead, it is the desires of the thought cells receiving new energy from the inner-plane weather. And if enough harmony can be added to them through harmonious thinking and feeling, in spite of any inner-plane weather or outer-plane condition, they will work for fortunate events. The details of thus using mental antidotes, conversion and rallying forces harmoniously to recondition the desires of the thought cells are set forth in chapter 8 (Serial Lesson 110), Course 10-1, *Delineating the Horoscope*.

However, the psychokinetic power of the thought cells is, on the average, only about one-half of the influence that determines the events that come into the life. Physical environment is commonly equally important. The physical environment may be such that when a progressed aspect forms the thought cells need exert only a little psychokinetic energy to bring the event they want into the life, or it may be such that any amount of psychokinetic energy cannot bring the event they want into the life. What happens is not the exclusive result of the psychokinetic power of the thought cells working for what they desire, and it is not the exclusive result of the physical environment. It is the algebraic sum of the psychokinetic power brought to bear minus the resistance of physical environment to that power. Therefore, in taking precautionary actions, if what the thought cells desire is also what the individual desires, he should do all he can to arrange the physical environment so they will have to use a minimum of psychokinetic energy to bring the event or condition they desire into the life. But if what the thought cells desire is what the individual does not desire, he should do all he can to arrange the physical environment so that no matter how much psychokinetic energy they bring to bear they cannot bring into the life the event or condition they desire.

What to Do Under Unfavorable Progressions Involving the Sun

To attract a more fortunate event than that otherwise indicated it is necessary that the thought cells in the astral body at each end of the stellar aerial mapped by the progressed aspect shall receive energy generated by the voluntary thoughts and feelings of such volume and harmony that they feel this energy more vividly than they feel the planetary energy coming in over the aerial mapped by the discordant aspect. And to reach the Sun terminal and influence its thought cells harmoniously, those thoughts and feelings must be associated with thoughts of dignity, courage, calm self-assurance, control and stamina.

When there are unfavorable progressions involving the Sun the power of the individual to mold affairs is in danger of being weakened by the discord stirred up among these controlling thought cells. And because these thought cells are intimately associated with the nerve currents and provide the electric vitality of the body, if they are permitted to do so they may become Rallying Forces that extend their influence into other departments of life than those reached by the aerial mapped by the aspect involving the Sun.

If the aspect involves a negative planet, thoughts and actions should be cultivated which are positive, and thus when harmoniously associated with thoughts of dignity, self-esteem, courage, control and stamina, tend to prevent depletion of the vital energy of the solar dynamic structure. But if the aspect involves a planet that tends toward unusual expansiveness and expenditure, the thoughts which should be held harmoniously in the mind in association with those of dignity, self-esteem, courage, and stamina should be those of deliberate control and calm confidence.

Unusual care should be given to dealing with the male sex, to political influences, to the attitude of those above one in station, to things affecting the honor and self-esteem, and especially as affecting the departments of life indicated by the houses in which the Sun and the other planet involved in the aspect are located.

When I say care, I do not mean fright. One of the most disastrous of human experiences is to be unwilling to face any condition that may come and carry on in spite of it.

I merely mean that far more foresight, skill and initiative are required at such a time than is customary to bring the same type of thing to a successful issue. Perhaps such scrutiny will bring the decision to abandon some attempt, or to write off as a loss something without carrying it further.

The Sun has no natural mental antidote, but the Religious thoughts are unusually potent when held in association with the Power thoughts. Whatever the thoughts are that are thus selected to be held in the mind at the same time as thoughts of power, of confidence and of ability to handle whatever situation arises, they must be held with a glow of enthusiasm. It is their harmony that must be depended upon to counteract the planetary discord being received.

What to Do Under Unfavorable Progressions Involving the Moon

Because the thought cells within the astral body mapped by the Moon in the birth chart, and by the progressed Moon, are so directly in contact with the magnetic energies of the electromagnetic form which determine the strength of the constitution and influence the nerve currents, progressed aspects involving the Moon are unusually significant. If given the opportunity, through the person responding in feeling to their influence, they readily become Rallying Forces which, reaching the other temporary stellar aerials and flowing over them into the other compartments of the astral body, may have an influence over many departments of life.

The thought cells of which the dynamic stellar structure mapped by the Moon chiefly is composed have had their origin in experiences with domestic life. Sympathy for the weak and helpless, for those in distress, and such impulses as relate to the preservation of the home and care for the family, and in a wider sense care for people everywhere who are less fortunate, or even care for plants and animals, are the type of feelings that directly reach the thought cells of the Moon dynamic structure within the astral body. Any thoughts, therefore, the purpose of which is to give so much harmonious energy to these stellar cells that the discordant energy reaching them from the planets is displaced, must be associated with sympathetic feelings of this kind.

Harmonious thinking and feeling in general, because the temporary stellar aerial having the Moon dynamic structure at one terminal is so open to reception, if associated with such feeling of desire and effort to minister to the welfare of others, tends to correct the discord of a progressed aspect involving the Moon. But the most effective thoughts and feelings for this purpose are of the Aggressive type ruled by Mars, which are the natural antidote.

In applying Mars thoughts and feelings care must be exercised that these express the constructive rather than the destructive tendencies. The energies received from a progressed aspect involving the Moon tend toward negativeness, receptivity and emotion. To apply the Aggressive thoughts successfully the feeling of positive constructive work must be maintained in association with the protection and welfare of others.

Irritation, anger, and other discordant thoughts only add increasing discord to the Domestic thought-cells. Negativeness and the feeling of frustration do likewise. But if a positive, yet constructive attitude is held, and the efforts are directed toward helping the weak or less fortunate, or toward protecting them, these harmonious thought energies will transform the Domestic thought compound into a compound the stellar cells of which will work from the inner plane to attract fortunate events.

Under unfavorable progressed aspects involving the Moon the health, contacts with women, relations with the public, the attitude of the mind, and those things indicated by the house position of the Moon and the other planet involved in the aspect should receive special attention.

What to Do Under Unfavorable Progressions Involving Mercury

The progressed aspects involving Mercury, as well as those involving Sun and Moon, add energy to stellar cells which have intimate contact with the electromagnetic form and the nerve currents. The nerve currents are largely directed by the objective thoughts which Mercury rules. And it is the natural function of these thoughts to tune electrical energies of the nervous system in temporarily on the frequency corresponding to the thoughts that thus gain attention. Thus the energies of Mercury commonly act as Rallying Forces, quite as strongly as those of Sun or Moon, to influence not merely the thought cells at the terminals of the temporary stellar aerial mapped by the aspect, but also to find their way into, and add their energy to, the terminals of other temporary stellar aerials which may be present.

Progressed aspects involving Mercury tend to give intensity and volume to thinking. When this thinking is too concentrated over a period of time, or is about unpleasant conditions, it causes great tension of the nervous system, and gives the thought cells at the terminals of the temporary stellar aerial discordant energy which enables them to attract unfortunate events into the life.

The house occupied by Mercury and the house occupied by the other planet involved in the aspect, together with the nature of that planet determine the type of thinking. Often the same train of thoughts, or those of similar context, is thought over and over again. Instead of such waste of mental energy, whatever problem is present should be thought through thoroughly and then dismissed by turning the attention to something else.

Good ideas and valuable discoveries often come under an unfavorable progressed aspect involving Mercury, and as good progress in study, in writing, or in other mental pursuits can be made under an unfavorable progressed aspect involving Mercury as can be made under a favorable progressed aspect. But if the ideas are expressed, writing is submitted for publication, or other persons are depended upon, the effect of the discord becomes quickly apparent.

Under an unfavorable progression involving Mercury only thoughts should be permitted which are pleasant and which move forward to some purpose. Clerical and other errors and slight mistakes should be guarded against, and especial care should be exercised as to the exact purport of any document which is signed. What is said to others also may be subject to misinterpretation.

The natural antidote, and thus the best type of thoughts to associate with the Intellectual activities at such a time are Religious thoughts. This does not signify one must turn to religion; but the optimism and confidence of Jupiter that all will work out as desired should be cultivated. The reliance on a higher power than human intelligence, after human intelligence has done its best, is an attitude which adds harmony to the thought cells influenced by Mercury in the most potent form.

What to Do Under Unfavorable Progressions Involving Venus

The progressed aspects involving Venus add energy to the thought cells which relate to the affections, and if this energy is discordant the thought cells thus given psychokinetic power bring events into the life that cause disappointment and grief through those toward whom there is, or it is desired there should be, a bond of attachment.

Under an unfavorable progression involving Venus slights, either real or fancied, are apt to arise. Perhaps events over which no one seems to have any control will, for the time being, cause conditions that stir up grief and emotion. The less attention the individual pays to slights during such a period the better. Whether intentional or not, and whether caused by unavoidable conditions or not, the discords of Venus thrive on emotional perturbation. The best procedure, therefore, is to invoke the aid of the Safety thoughts, ruled by Saturn, and also sufficient of the Power thoughts, ruled by the Sun.

The Safety thoughts, which give a cold appraisal of circumstances, and are under the dominion of reason and quite apart from emotion, are the natural antidote for the Social thoughts of Venus. That is, they enter into the Social thought-cells in the astral body most readily in the formation of a highly beneficial compound. And the realization that the less emotion permitted the less misfortune will be experienced, is an easy way to apply these Safety thoughts. Pleasure should be felt in this conquest of emotion by cold reason.

Because Venus is the planet of joy and mirth, as well as of art, music and social pleasure, one who has considerable resolution, and can call forth the stamina and self-esteem of the Power thoughts to overlook emotional hurt, often can make even severely unfavorable progressed aspects involving Venus subject to Conversion (see chapter 8 (Serial Lesson 110), Course 10-1, *Delineating the Horoscope*), and thus gain much benefit from them.

What to Do Under Unfavorable Progressions Involving Mars

As a progressed aspect involving Mars is always present when an accident takes place, and when an infection is contracted, and as it is the planet of haste and strife, the least exposure to danger and infection, and the greater the avoidance of haste and strife, within reason, the better. Often, under such discord a fight is thrust upon one in such a manner that measures for self protection become necessary.

We cannot say that because Mars is involved in an unfavorable progressed aspect that an ill person should not have an operation. Not infrequently such an operation is the only measure that will save the life. And either a favorable or an unfavorable progressed aspect involving Mars is always present at the time of a surgical operation. Nor can we lay down a blanket rule that a person under an unfavorable aspect involving Mars should refuse to fight, as it may be the only manner in which invasion of his rights can be prevented. But if conditions permit the operation to be postponed, and if the individual can avoid a fight without too great sacrifice, it is better to wait for more favorable progressed aspects under which to solve such difficulties.

Under unfavorable progressions involving Mars it is better to avoid danger; but if danger comes, as it often does, to face it with courage, resolution and calmness is the best way to mitigate its effect. Machines and mechanical contrivances are apt to break or get out of order more readily than usual. Fire hazards increase, and too great energy expenditures threaten.

Haste, impulse, and too great activity should be guarded against. But as Mars is a Social planet, the relations with people are even more commonly a source of difficulty. Pains should be taken not to say or do that which causes offense or which will lead to strife, unless it has calmly been decided upon that strife is the only proper course to pursue.

Because Aggressive thoughts will come so spontaneously into the mind no special effort toward associating other thoughts with them is necessary. The Domestic thoughts are the natural antidote, and the best way of applying them is merely to interest oneself as thoroughly as possible in helping those who are weak and in distress. This maternal attitude and the actions springing from it, if sufficiently encouraged, will generate the thought elements which, if pleasure is felt in them, will combine with the Aggressive thoughts in the astral body to form a more fortunate compound. The more such thoughts of helping others tend to displace the discordant thoughts of strife the more favorable the events which will be attracted by the progressed aspect. Under Mars inner-plane weather cultivate patience and take it easy.

What to Do Under Unfavorable Progressions Involving Jupiter

Self-indulgence, extravagance, unwise optimism, too great generosity, unwillingness to consider the cost, and unwarranted business expansion are the chief things which an unfavorable progression involving Jupiter tends to attract.

All these things are attracted due to lack of careful analysis of the situation, the reliance upon chance or the opinions of others, or on the good offices of others. Sometimes even too great enthusiasm to present one's religious opinions may cause difficulty.

But whatever the discord that a progressed aspect involving Jupiter brings, basically it is due to lack of Intelligence. The house position of Jupiter and of the other planet involved in the aspect indicate the departments of life chiefly affected; but in general, as Jupiter is a Business planet, the finances also need attention. And the kind of attention most needed is to cultivate a pleasure in carefully analyzing and appraising by the most conservative methods every transaction which is entered into, especially those indicated by the progressed aspect.

The Intellectual thoughts are the natural antidote to the thought elements given activity by Jupiter progressed aspects; and by taking pleasure in applying intelligence and care to the activities is the best method of converting them into a compound which will attract fortunate events.

What to Do Under Unfavorable Progressions Involving Saturn

The trend of the thoughts under an unfavorable progression involving Saturn is to look upon the dark side of things. The planetary vibrations received by the thought cells at the terminals of the temporary stellar aerial are heavy, morose, self-centered and lacking in buoyancy and elasticity; imparting to these cells a feeling which causes them to work from the inner plane to attract want, responsibility and loss.

These vibrations are negative, and to correct this negativeness, and prevent the development of fear, timidity and the tendency to worry, the Power thoughts of the Sun should be cultivated by holding thoughts of courage, determination and stamina. But of even more benefit, as they are the natural antidote for the Safety thoughts of Saturn, a deliberate effort should be made to encourage the Social thoughts.

Safeguarding the interests through positive action, rather than through negative fear, frequently is necessary under afflictions involving Saturn. That is, commonly it is unwise to press into activity the departments of life influenced by an unfavorable progressed aspect involving Saturn during the time the aspect is within the one degree of effective orb; but rather to turn for the time being to other, and less discordant interests.

Because Saturn thoughts are so insistently present, weighing down the personality, no special effort is necessary to cause them to associate with other thoughts and feelings that may be cultivated. Yet social contacts and other Venus activities are of no value unless the light-heartedness and gaiety of Venus are experienced. It may require great fortitude, when things apparently are going to pieces, and even social slights and financial losses may be in the offing, to mix with people, to dance, sing, go to the movies, make merry and take joy in art and music. But there is nothing better to drive away the Saturn blues, and nothing better to add happy thought elements to the Safety thought compounds in a manner which most readily transforms them into a dynamic stellar compound which attracts good fortune. Under Saturn inner-plane weather keep your chin up and cultivate cheerfulness.

What to Do Under Unfavorable Progressions Involving Uranus

Uranus, as octave of Mercury, has direct access to the electromagnetic form through the nerve currents; and its discords tend to unusually high tension of the nervous system, and to depletion of the electromagnetic energy. In particular it opens the gate to outside influences, notably those of people, who often gain at such times, through hypnotic effect, mental influence, or through misplaced confidence, altogether too great control over the life.

MAJOR PROGRESSIONS OF THE PLANETS

If this be recognized, that attachments made under progressed aspects involving Uranus seldom are lasting, and that such misfortune as the influence brings is in some manner due to a human agency, it will enable the individual to guard against difficulties. It is the sudden and unexpected which happens under progressed aspects involving Uranus.

New contrivances, such as radios, automobiles, and intricate machines, especially those depending in some manner on electricity, tend to get out of order under unfavorable progressions involving Uranus. All attachments made during such a progression should be subject to certain reservations. Yet excellent progress in astrology and the occult sciences can be made under even heavy unfavorable progressed aspects involving this planet. An aspect involving Uranus favors gaining new information; and as a result of such new information the viewpoint often is changed.

The natural antidote for an unfavorable Uranus is the same as for unfavorable Mercury. What has been said as to applying the Religious thoughts to counteract a discordant Mercury applies with equal force to transforming a Uranian thought-compound into one of more fortunate trend.

What to Do Under Unfavorable Progressions Involving Neptune

An unfavorable progression involving Neptune requires the same cultivation of the Safety thoughts as that prescribed for its octave, Venus. But in addition, because it is so much more negative and sensitive, the Power thoughts should receive even more consideration. Courage, stamina, positiveness and determination are especially required to offset the shrinking sensitiveness and the dreaminess which the vibrations of Neptune encourage.

Such discord tends to attract schemes which work to the detriment of the individual. Imaginary advantages seem unusually attractive, and may lead to loss. On the other hand, imaginary dangers may harass, and require adequate Power thoughts to banish. Psychic matters, new habits, or even drugs may tend to enslave the person and poison may affect the health; yet even under quite unfavorable progressed aspects involving Neptune good progress may be made in music, in fiction writing, or in dramatic work.

With these additional considerations, what has been said under unfavorable progressions involving Venus applies with equal force to unfavorable progressions involving Neptune.

What to Do Under Unfavorable Progressions Involving Pluto

The Domestic thoughts of the Moon apparently are expanded in the octave expression, Pluto, to embrace society as a whole. As octave of the Moon, the vibrations of Pluto have ready access to the nerve currents, and more readily than any other planetary influence tune the organism in on thoughts radiated by intelligences of either plane.

On its better side Pluto has to do with Soul Mates; and on its adverse side with weakness due to separation. Unusual discrimination is required while an unfavorable progression of Pluto is operative that contact with the criminal world of both planes be avoided kidnapping, or becoming the tool of visible or invisible racketeers, should specially be guarded against. Such things at times are present in slight degree without being recognized. Association with groups of doubtful character, and situations that might lead to coercion, should be avoided.

The Aggressive thoughts, as natural antidotes, should be applied under unfavorable progressions involving Pluto in precisely the same manner advocated for unfavorable progressions involving the Moon.

What to Do Under Unfavorable Progressions Involving the M.C.

A progressed aspect involving the M.C. forms a temporary stellar aerial between the dynamic stellar structure mapped by the planet and this broadcasting station. The chief energy picked up is that of the planet involved. Therefore use the instructions given under the heading what to do when this planet is under unfavorable progressions, and associate the thoughts there indicated as harmoniously as possible with thoughts relating to honor, business and publicity. And take pains to see to it that the behavior and physical environment offer as much resistance as possible to any effort made by the M.C. thought-cells to bring unfavorable publicity, loss of position, or business adversity into the life.

What to Do Under Unfavorable Progressions Involving the Asc.

A progressed aspect involving the Asc. forms a temporary stellar aerial between the dynamic stellar structure mapped by the planet and this ground wire. The chief energy picked up is that of the planet involved. Therefore use the instructions given under the heading what to do when this planet is under unfavorable progressions, and associate the thoughts there indicated as strongly and as harmoniously as possible with thoughts relating to the health, the personality and personal affairs. And take pains to see to it that the behavior and the physical environment, including the diet, are the proper precautionary actions for such physical illness as the Birth-Chart Constants and the Progressed Constants, as set forth in Course 16, *Stellar Healing*, at the time indicate might possibly develop.

MAJOR PROGRESSIONS OF THE PLANETS 77

Calculating Aspects Made by Major-Progressed Planets

Major-progressed aspects involving the planets are calculated in exactly the same way as are major-progressed aspects of Sun, examples of which are given in chapter 2 (Serial Lesson 111), and as are major-progressed aspects made by the Moon, examples of which are given in chapter 3 (Serial Lesson 112).

And the time an aspect moves to within the one degree of effective orb, and therefore first commences to have an influence, and the time an aspect moves past the one degree of effective orb, and thus loses its influence, are calculated in precisely the same way, except that the gap to be closed is indicated by the position one degree before or one degree past the perfect aspect.

FRACTIONS OF A MONTH: When working progressions by proportion there often is a fraction of a month to be converted into days. To do this multiply the numerator by 30 and divide the product by the denominator. Thus in example 1 below there are 21/73 months. Multiplying 21 by 30 gives 630. Dividing 630 by 73 gives 9 days.

The examples which follow all relate to Chart 3a, given on page 66. The chart is erected for June 28, 1920, 12:23 p.m. CST. 89W. 40:40N. The EGMT is plus 6h 23m. The Limiting Date is March 22, 1920.

Example 1. Venus sextile Saturn r: Ephemeris date June 30, 1920, Venus is (b) 20' past the aspect, and moving daily (a) 1° 13', or 73'. By proportion, multiplying (b) 20 by (c) 12 (months) gives 240. Dividing 240 by (a) 73 gives (d) 3 21/73 months, or 3 mo 9d. June 30, 1920, is 2 days after the L.D. and thus Map. D. for 1922. Subtracting the 3 months, 9 days from March 22, 1922, gives Venus sextile Saturn r December 13, 1921. By logarithms, the problem is worked in detail on page 2 of chapter 1 (Serial Lesson 19).

Example 2. Venus applying sextile Saturn r within one degree of orb: To reach the one degree of effective orb Venus must reach 6 Cancer 06. Ephemeris date June 29, 1920, Venus is 6 Cancer 13 and thus (b) 7' past the required position, and moving daily (a) 1° 14', or 74'. By proportion, multiplying (b) 7 by (c) 12 gives 84. Dividing 84 by (a) 74 gives (d) 1 10/74 months, or 1 mo 4d.

By logarithms, subtracting log. (a) 1.2891 from log. (b) 2.3133 gives 1.0242, which is the log. of (d) 2h 16m. Dividing the 2 by 2 gives 1mo. Dividing the 16 and 4 gives 4d. June 29, 1920, is Map. D. for calendar year 1921. Subtracting the 1 month, 4 days found by either method from March 22, 1921, gives Venus applying sextile Saturn r within one degree of orb February 18, 1921.

Example 3. Venus separating sextile Saturn r within one degree of orb: To leave the one degree of effective orb Venus must be more than 8 Cancer 06. Ephemeris date July 1, 1920, Venus is 8 Cancer 40 and thus (b) 34' past the required position, and moving daily (a) 1° 14', or 74'. By proportion, multiplying (b) 34 by (c) 12 gives 408. Dividing 408 by (a) 74 gives (d) 5 38/74 months, or 5mo 15d.

By logarithms, subtracting log. (a) 1.2891 from log. (b) 1.6269 gives .3378, which is the log. of 11h 02m. Dividing the 11 by 2 gives 5mo with a remainder of 60m. Adding the 60m to the 2m gives 62m. Dividing the 62 by 4 gives 15d. July 1, 1920, is Map. D. for calendar year 1923. Subtracting the 5 months, 15 days found by either method from March 22, 1923, gives Venus separating sextile Saturn r within one degree of orb, after which its effect is negligible, October 7, 1922.

Example 4. Venus square Mars p: Ephemeris date July 22, 1920, shows Mars 5 Scorpio 05 and Venus 4 Leo 30 and thus (b) 35' from square aspect. Venus is moving daily 1° 14' while Mars moves 28'. The difference is the gain (a) 46'. By proportion, multiplying (b) 35 by (a) 12 gives 420. Dividing 420 by 46 gives (d) 9 6/46 months, or 9mo 4d.

By logarithms, subtracting log. (a) 1.4956 from log. (b) 1.6143 gives .1187, which is the log. of (d) 18h 16m. Dividing the 18 by 2 gives 9mo. Dividing the 16 by 4 gives 4d. July 22 is 24 days after the L.D., and is thus Map. D. for calendar year 1944. Adding the 9 months, 4 days found by either method to March 22, 1944, gives Venus square Mars p December 26, 1944.

Example 5. Venus applying square Mars p within one degree of orb: Ephemeris date July 21, 1920, shows Mars 4 Scorpio 37 and Venus 3 Leo 17, and thus lacking (b) 20' of being within the one degree orb of the square. Venus is moving daily 1° 13' and Mars is moving 28'. The difference is the daily gain (a) 45'. By proportion, multiplying (b) 20 by (c) 12 gives 240. Dividing 240 by (a) 45 gives (d) 5 15/45 months, or 5 mo 10d.

By logarithms, subtracting log. (a) 1.5051 from log. (b) 1.8573 gives .3522, which is the log. of (d) 10h 40m. Dividing the 10 by 2 gives 5mo. Dividing the 40 by 4 gives 10d. July 21, 1920, is Map. D. for calendar year 1943. Adding the 5 months, 10 days found by either method to March 22, 1943, gives Venus applying square Mars p within one degree of orb September 2, 1943.

Example 6. Venus separating square Mars p within one degree of orb: Ephemeris date July 24, 1920, shows Mars 6 Scorpio 01 and Venus 6 Leo 58, and thus lacking (b) 3' of being one degree past the square aspect. Venus is moving daily 1° 14' and Mars is moving 29'. The difference is the daily gain (a) 45'. By proportion, multiplying (b) 3 by (c) 12 gives 36. Dividing 36 by 45 gives (d) 36/45 months, or 24d.

By logarithms, subtracting log. (a) 1.5051 from log. (b) 2.6812 gives 1.1761, which is the log. of (d) 1h 36m, or 96m. Dividing the 96 by 4 gives 24d. July 24,

MAJOR PROGRESSIONS OF THE PLANETS

1920, is Map.D. for calendar year 1946. Adding the 24 days found by either method to March 22, 1946, gives Venus separating square Mars p within one degree of orb, after which its influence is negligible, April 16, 1946.

Example 7. Saturn sextile Pluto r: Ephemeris date June 30, 1920, Saturn is (b) 1' past the aspect. Saturn is moving daily (a) 5'. By proportion, multiplying (b) 1 by (c) 12 gives 12. Dividing 12 by (a) 5 gives (d) 2 2/5 months, or 2mo 12d.

By logarithms, subtracting log. (a) 2.4594 from log. (b) 3.1584 gives .6990, which is the log. of (d) 4h 48m. Dividing the 4 by 2 gives 2mo. Dividing the 48 by 4 gives 12d. June 30, 1920, is Map.D. for calendar year 1922. Subtracting the 2mo 12d found by either method from March 22, 1922, gives Saturn sextile Pluto r January 10, 1922.

Example 8. Venus conjunction M.C. r: Ephemeris date July 4, 1920, Venus is 12 Cancer 21 and thus (b) 7' past the aspect. Venus is moving daily (a) 1° 13', or 73'. By proportion, multiplying (b) 7 by (c) 12 gives 84. Dividing 84 by (a) 73 gives (d) 1 11/73 months, or 1mo 5d.

By logarithms, subtracting log. (a) 1.2950 from log. (b) 2.3133 gives 1.0183, which is the log. of (d) 2h 18m. Dividing the 2 by 2 gives 1mo. Dividing the 18 by 4 gives 5d. July 4, 1920, is Map. D. for calendar year 1926. Subtracting the 1 month, 5 days found by either method from March 22, 1926, gives Venus conjunction M.C. r February 17, 1926.

Example 9. Mercury trine Moon r: Ephemeris date July 6, 1920, Mercury lacks (b) 5' of the aspect, and is moving daily (a) 30'. By proportion, multiplying (b) 5 by (a) 12 gives 60. Dividing 60 by (a) 30 gives (d) 2mo.

By logarithms, subtracting log. (a) 1.6812 from log. (b) 2.4594 gives .7782, which is the log. of (d) 4h. Dividing the 4 by 2 gives 2mo. July 6, 1920, is Map. D. for calendar year 1928. Adding the 2 months found by either method to March 22, 1928, gives Mercury trine Moon r May 22, 1928.

Example 10. Mercury conjunction Neptune r: Ephemeris date July 10, 1920, Mercury lacks (b) 4' of the aspect, and is moving daily (a) 12'. By proportion, multiplying (b) 4 by (c) 12 gives 48. Dividing 48 by (a) 12 gives 4mo.

By logarithms, subtracting log. (a) 2.0792 from log. (b) 2.5563 gives .4771, which is the log. of (d) 8h. Dividing the 8 by 2 gives 4mo. July 10, 1920, is Map. D. for calendar year 1932. Adding the 4 months found by either method to March 22, 1932, gives Mercury conjunction Neptune r July 22, 1932.

Example 11. Venus sesquisquare Uranus r: Ephemeris date July 11, 1920, Venus is (b) 26' past the aspect, and is moving daily (a) 1° 14', or 74'. By proportion, multiplying (b) 26 by (c) 12 gives 312. Dividing 312 by (a) 74 gives (d) 4 16/74 months, or 4mo 6d.

By logarithms, subtracting log. (a) 1.2891 from log. (b) 1.7434 gives .4543, which is log. of (d) 8h 26m. Dividing the 8 by 2 gives 4mo. Dividing the 26 by 4 gives 6d. July 11, 1920, is Map. D. for calendar year 1933. Subtracting the 4 months, 6 days found by either method from March 22, 1933, gives Venus sesquisquare Uranus r November 16, 1932.

Example 12. Mars square Mercury r: Ephemeris date July 16, 1920, Mars is (b) 1' past the aspect, and is moving daily (a) 26'. By proportion, multiplying (b) 1 by (c) 12 gives 12. Dividing 12 by (a) 26 gives (d) 12/26 months, or 14d.

By logarithms, subtracting log. (a) 1.7434 from log. (b) 3.1584 gives 1.4150, which is the log. of (d) 55m. Dividing the 55 by 4 gives 14d. July 16, 1920, is Map. D. for calendar year 1938. Subtracting the 14 days found by either method from March 22, 1938, gives Mars square Mercury r March 8, 1938.

Example 13. Mercury parallel Mars p: Ephemeris date July 18, 1920, Mars has declination 13 S 50 and gains declination 10' per day, while Mercury has declination 13 N 59 and loses declination 5' per day. The aspect lacks (b) 9'. As they are moving toward each other by declination we add 10 and 5 which gives the daily gain as (a) 15'. By proportion, multiplying (9) by (c) 12 gives 108. Dividing 108 by (a) 15 gives (d) 7 3/15 months, or 7mo 6d.

By logarithms, subtracting log. (a) 1.9823 from log. (b) 2.2041 gives .2218, which is the log. of (d) 14h 24m. Dividing the 14 by 2 gives 7mo. Dividing the 24 by 4 gives 6d. July 18, 1920, is Map. D. for calendar year 1940. Adding the 7 months, 6 days found by either method to March 22, 1940, gives Mercury parallel Mars p October 28, 1940.

Example 14. Mercury applying parallel Mars p within one degree of orb: Ephemeris date July 12, 1920, Mars has declination 13 S 21 and gains declination 9' per day, and Mercury has declination 14 N 23 and loses declination 10' per day. They lack (b) 2' of being within the one degree of effective orb. As they are moving toward each other by declination we add the 9 and 10 which gives the daily gain as (a) 19'. By proportion, multiplying (b) 2 by (c) 12 gives 24. Dividing 24 by (a) 19 gives (d) 1 5/19 months, or 1mo 8d.

By logarithms, subtracting log. (a) 1.8796 from log. (b) 2.8573 gives .9777, which is the log. of (d) 2h 32m. Dividing the 2 by 2 gives 1mo. Dividing the 32 by 4 gives 8d. July 15, 1920, is Map. D. for calendar year 1937. Adding the 1 month, 8 days found by either method to March 22, 1937, gives Mercury applying parallel Mars p within one degree of orb April 30, 1937.

Example 15. Mercury separating parallel Mars *p* within one degree of orb: Ephemeris date August 18, 1920, Mars is declination 19 S 10 and gains in declination 10' per day, while Mercury is declination 18 N 20 and loses declination 7' per day. As they are moving toward each other by declination we add the 10 and 7 which gives the daily gain as (a) 17'. They lack (b) 10' of being one degree past the parallel aspect. By proportion, multiplying (b) 10 by (c) 12 gives 120. Dividing 120 by (a) 17 gives (d) 7 1/17 months, or 7 mo 2d.

By logarithms, subtracting log. (a) 1.9279 from log. (b) 2.1584 gives .2305, which is the log. of (d) 14h 7m. Dividing the 14 by 2 gives 7mo. Dividing the 7 by 4 gives 2d. August 18, 1920, is Map. D. for calendar year 1971. Adding the 7 months, 2 days found by either method to March 22, 1971, gives Mercury separating parallel Mars *p* one degree of orb October 24, 1971.

Example 16. Mars trine Venus *r*: Ephemeris date July 22, 1920, Mars lacks (b) 14' of the aspect, and moves daily (a) 28'. By proportion, multiplying (b) 14 by (c) 12 gives 168. Dividing 168 by (a) 28 gives (d) 6mo.

By logarithms, subtracting log. (a) 1.7112 from log. (b) 2.0122 gives .3010, which is the log. of (d) 12h. Dividing the 12 by 2 gives 6mo. July 22, 1920, is Map. D. for calendar year 1944. Adding the 6 months, found by either method to March 22, 1944, gives Mars trine Venus *r* September 22, 1944.

Example 17. Mars trine Sun *r*: Ephemeris date July 25, 1920, Mars lacks (b) 12' of the aspect and moves daily (a) 29'. By proportion, multiplying (b) 12 by (c) 12 gives 144. Dividing 144 by (a) 29 gives (d) 4 28/29 months, or 4mo 29d.

By logarithms, subtracting log. (a) 1.6969 from log. (b) 2.0792 gives .3823, which is the log. of (d) 9h 57m. Dividing the 9 by 2 gives 4mo with a remainder of 60m. Adding the 60m to the 57m gives 117m. Dividing the 117 by 4 gives 29d. July 25, 1920, is Map. D. for calendar year 1947. Adding the 4 months, 29 days found by either method to March 22, 1947, gives Mars trine Sun *r* August 21, 1947.

Example 18. Mercury conjunction Mercury *r*: Ephemeris date July 29, 1920, Mercury lacks (b) 2' of the aspect, and is moving retrograde daily (a) 39'. Multiplying (b) 2 by (c) 12 gives 24. Dividing 24 by (a) 39 gives (d) 24/39 months, or 18d.

By logarithms, subtracting log. (a) 1.5673 from log. (b) 2.8573 gives 1.2900, which is the log. of (d) 1h 14m, or 74m. Dividing the 74 by 4 gives 18d. July 29, 1920, is Map. D. for calendar year 1951. Adding the 18 days found by either method to March 22, 1951, gives Mercury conjunction Mercury *r* April 10, 1951.

Example 19. Venus parallel Saturn r: birth-chart Saturn is 10 N 35. Ephemeris date August 17, 1920, Venus decreasing declination is 10 N 27 and thus (b) 8' past the aspect, and moving daily (a) 27'. By proportion, multiplying (b) 8 by (c) 12 gives 96. Dividing 96 by (a) 27 gives (d) 3 15/27 months, or 3mo 17d.

By logarithms, subtracting log. (a) 1.7270 from log. (b) 2.2553 gives .5283, which is the log. of (d) 7h 7m. Dividing the 7 by 2 gives 3mo with a remainder of 60m. Adding the 60m to the 7m gives 67m. Dividing the 67 by 4 gives 17d. August 17, 1920, is Map. D. for calendar year 1970. Subtracting the 3 months, 17 days found by either method from March 22, 1970, gives Venus parallel Saturn r December 5, 1969.

Chapter 5

Minor Progressions of Sun and Angles

Serial Lesson Number 114
Original Copyright, 1934
Elbert Benjamine
a.k.a. C. C. Zain

Copyright 2014, The Church of Light

MINOR PROGRESSION DATE TABLE

Years Age	Y.	Mo.	Days	Years Age	Y.	Mo.	Days
1	00	00	27	25	01	10	18
2	00	01	25	26	01	11	15
3	00	02	22	27	02	00	07
4	00	03	19	28	02	01	04
5	00	04	17	29	02	02	02
6	00	05	14	30	02	02	29
7	00	06	11	31	02	03	26
8	00	07	08	32	02	04	24
9	00	08	06	33	02	05	21
10	00	09	03	34	02	06	18
11	00	10	00	35	02	07	16
12	00	10	28	36	02	08	13
13	00	11	25	37	02	09	10
14	01	00	17	38	02	10	07
15	01	01	15	39	02	11	05
16	01	02	12	40	02	11	29
17	01	03	09	41	03	00	24
18	01	04	06	42	03	01	22
19	01	05	04	43	03	02	19
20	01	06	01	44	03	03	16
21	01	06	28	45	03	04	14
22	01	07	26	46	03	05	11
23	01	08	23	47	03	06	08
24	01	09	20	48	03	07	05

Computed by W. M. A. Drake

MINOR PROGRESSION DATE TABLE

Years Age	Y.	Mos.	Days	Years Age	Y.	Mos.	Days
49	03	08	03	73	05	05	18
50	03	09	00	74	05	06	15
51	03	09	27	75	05	07	13
52	03	10	25	76	05	08	10
53	03	11	22	77	05	09	07
54	04	00	14	78	05	10	04
55	04	01	12	79	05	11	02
56	04	02	09	80	05	11	29
57	04	03	06	81	06	00	21
58	04	04	03	82	06	01	19
59	04	05	01	83	06	02	16
60	04	05	28	84	06	03	13
61	04	06	25	85	06	04	11
62	04	07	23	86	06	05	08
63	04	08	20	87	06	06	05
64	04	09	17	88	06	07	02
65	04	10	15	89	06	07	30
66	04	11	12	90	06	08	27
67	05	00	04	91	06	09	24
68	05	01	01	92	06	10	22
69	05	01	29	93	06	11	19
70	05	02	26	94	07	00	11
71	05	03	23	95	07	01	09
72	05	04	21	96	07	02	06

Computed by W. M. A. Drake

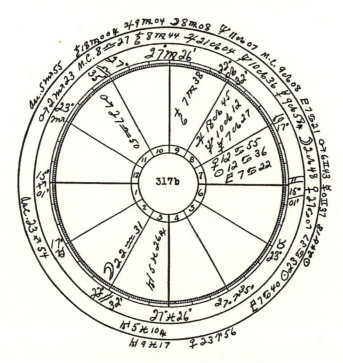

Minors: Birth Chart 317b

July 4, 1920, 5:00 p.m. CST. 90W. 30N.
L.D. Jan. 19, 1920. M.C.C. minus 2S 14° 50'
S.C. minus 7S 9° 55'. 1932 Mip. D. May 28, 1921

*Major progressions in outer circle for Jan. 19, 1932
Minor progressions outside chart for Jan. 19, 1932.*

1932 Feb. 18   Asc. *m* parallel Mercury *p*.

1932 March 1   Sun *m* sextile Venus *p*.

1932 March 24   Asc. *m* square Mercury *p*.

1932 March 29   Asc. *m* square Neptune *r*.

1932 May 28   M.C. *m* parallel Jupiter *p*.

1932 Sept. 26   Sun *m* sesquisquare Mars *r*.

1932 Dec. 12   M.C. *m* sextile Mars *p*.

Chapter 5

Minor Progressions of Sun and Angles

MINOR progressed aspects have two distinct influences. They exert a power, and a harmony or discord, 1/27.3 of the power and harmony or discord of the same aspect between the same two planets when made by major-progressed aspect. The psychokinetic power of the thought cells receiving new energy through minor-progressed aspects thus enables them to attract into the life minor events. Minor events coincide with characteristic minor-progressed aspects.

But in addition to this independent influence, if the minor-progressed aspect is to one of the terminals (as both birth-chart and progressed positions are terminals, unless a planet aspects its birth-chart place each progressed aspect has four terminals) of a major-progressed aspect, it steps up, and thus reinforces the major-progressed aspect. So far as effects are concerned, it seems to operate on the major-progressed power as an automobile induction coil operates in stepping up the battery current to sufficient voltage to afford the spark necessary for ignition. And for a major-progressed aspect to gain enough power to attract a major event it would seem that it is as necessary for it to be thus reinforced by a minor-progressed aspect to one of its four terminals as it is for an automobile to have its battery current stepped up by an induction coil to get satisfactory ignition.

Church of Light statistical studies of the major and minor-progressed aspects in many hundreds of charts at the time some major event took place demonstrate that major events take place only when the characteristic major-progressed aspect is thus reinforced by a minor-progressed aspect. These statistical studies indicate that this reinforcement effect seems to have no influence whatever on the harmony or discord of the major-progressed aspect. But it does apparently step up whatever power the major-progressed aspect has at the time by the same percentage a similar major-progressed aspect steps up the birth-chart power of the planets involved. Thus during the time a major-progressed aspect is within its one effective degree of orb there are sure to be several lesser periods during which minor-progressed aspects step it up. And whatever major event occurs is sure to happen on one of these peaks of power.

As is explained in chapter 7 (Serial Lesson 116), in addition to the minor-progressed aspect to one of its terminals, there must also be a transit aspect to one of its terminals at the precise time an event attracted by a major-progressed aspect enters the life. But relative to the reinforcing power of minor-progressed aspects, extensive statistical research fully justifies the following:

RULE: The Major-Progressed Constants of an event or disease are always reinforced by a minor-progressed aspect heavier than from the Moon to one of its four terminals at the time the event occurs or the disease develops.

This rule is very important, for it enables us to eliminate the possibility of a given event or the development of a given disease, even during those periods when the Major-Progressed Constants are within the one degree of effective orb, except during those limited periods when ALL these Major-Progressed Constants are reinforced by minor-progressed aspects.

But thus to be sure they are eliminated during a given period, not only the zodiacal minor-progressed position of the ten planets and the M.C. and Asc. must be precisely ascertained, but the declinations also of all twelve minor-progressed positions. Using a Lunar Constant for such calculations may give an error of from one to three days, which is not significant in timing minor events. But during three days minor-progressed Sun, Mercury and Venus may each move not less than 15'. Thus this margin of error may make it appear that they are not within orb of an aspect when in reality they are. And should an individual undertake some dangerous exploit during a heavy discordant major-progressed aspect involving Mars, under the impression there was no minor-progressed aspect within one degree of perfect involving Mars, when in reality there thus was, this error might cost him his life. Or the error may indicate that there is a minor-progressed aspect within one degree of orb to the terminal of a major-progressed aspect when in reality there is not. On the assumption the minor-progressed aspect is thus exerting reinforcing power, an individual under the influence of some favorable major-progressed aspect may undertake some venture and fail, in which he would have been successful had the minor-progressed aspect actually been within the one degree of effective orb. Thus on certain occasions it is essential to be able to determine quite precisely when a minor-progressed aspect is, and when it is not, within the one degree of effective orb to a birth-chart or major-progressed position.

The above rule enables us more precisely to time indicated events; for the event will occur on one of the peaks of power indicated when ALL the Major-Progressed Constants are reinforced by minor-progressed aspects.

As indicated on page 148 of chapter 8 (Serial Lesson 117), it greatly aids in rectifying charts; because if the chart is correct it will have not only a major-progressed aspect to the ruler of the house mapping the department of life affected by the event, and the Major-Progressed Constants of the event—often involving the rulers of several houses—at the time the event occurs, but as an additional check, the major-progressed aspect indicating the event in each case must be reinforced by a minor-progressed aspect and released by a transit aspect.

If the ruler of the house mapping the department of life affected by the major-progressed aspect, and each of the other Major-Progressed Constants, are not thus reinforced by a minor-progressed aspect and released by a transit-progressed aspect at the time of the event, the house positions of the chart are not correct.

There are still other important applications of the rule given above, but undoubtedly its greatest usefulness is in the selection of the best time to do things. Commonly, minor-progressed aspects last only a short period. Therefore, during the time a major-progressed aspect is within its one degree of effective orb, it usually is possible to select several short periods during which no minor-progressed aspect to any of its terminals reinforces it. If one were compelled to do something hazardous, such as take a dangerous trip, during the time there was an unfavorable major-progressed aspect involving Mars, if one selected a time when this major-progressed aspect was not reinforced by a minor-progressed aspect, the danger would be reduced, if not to nil, at least to a minimum. Thus far in analyzing several hundred accidents we have found none unless a major-progressed aspect involving Mars was reinforced by one or more minor-progressed aspect.

On the other hand, if one wished to do something at a time when it was essential to get all the benefit possible from a favorable major-progressed aspect, one could select a time when several minor-progressed aspects were reinforcing the major-progressed aspect. Often it is possible to find a short period during which the reinforcements give the major-progressed aspect several times its normal peak power. The power to bring the desired event to pass during such a short period would consequently be much more than when no reinforcement was present.

Most major events do not drop unheralded out of the blue. Commonly there are preliminary minor occurrences leading up to the major event, and after the major event is past quite frequently there are minor occurrences resulting from it. The minor events leading to, and resulting from, a major event are indicated and timed by minor-progressed aspects involving one or more of the terminals of the major-progressed aspect indicating the major event. This knowledge may be quite valuable in anticipating the kind of major event that is approaching, and in anticipating the time certain conditions developing from it will occur.

Minor-Progressed Aspects are of Value Only When Made to Birth-Chart Planets or to Major-Progressed Planets

Experience proves that the aspects among themselves of minor-progressed planets afford so little energy that their influence should be neglected.

Any calendar time interval can be converted into minor-progressed time interval, and any minor-progressed time interval can be converted into calendar time interval, at the rate of 27.3 days minor progression time being equivalent to one year of calendar time, and 360° movement of the Moon by minor progression being equivalent to one year (365.25 days) of calendar time. The ephemeris Moon thus moves by minor progression approximately 1 degree a day.

To be precise, the minor-progressed Moon moves exactly the same number of degrees and minutes as the transiting Sun. Thus the zodiacal distance between the birth-chart Sun and the birth-chart Moon is at all times the precise zodiacal distance between the minor-progressed Moon and the transiting Sun. Therefore, from the transiting Sun—the position of the Sun in the ephemeris on any given calendar date—the position of minor-progressed Moon may easily be found, and from the position of the minor-progressed Moon the minor-progressed positions of the other planets may be ascertained. And from the position of the minor-progressed Moon when any minor-progressed aspect is formed the transiting position of the Sun may easily be found, and from the transiting position of the Sun, by looking in an ephemeris for this position of the Sun, the calendar day the minor-progressed aspect is formed can be ascertained. If desired, by calculating the time on that day when the Sun reaches the precise ' of the indicated position, the time on that calendar day when the aspect is formed also can be ascertained. The zodiacal distance between the birth-chart Moon and the birth-chart Sun, used in these calculations, is called the Solar Constant.

Finding the Solar Constant

The Solar Constant (abbreviated S.C.) is the zodiacal distance in the chart of birth between the Moon and the Sun in signs, °s, and 's, expressed as plus or minus, so that when added to the sign, °, and ' occupied by the Moon, the algebraic sum gives the sign, °, and ' occupied by the Sun.

To find the Solar Constant, from the larger zodiacal longitude in signs, °s and 's occupied by the Sun or Moon in the birth chart, subtract the smaller zodiacal longitude in signs, °s and 's occupied by Sun or Moon in the birth chart. Place before the signs, °s and 's so found the plus or minus sign indicating whether these are to be added to, or subtracted from, the place occupied by the Moon to ascertain the place occupied by the Sun.

Then, wherever the Moon may be by minor progression, algebraically add the sign, °, and ' it occupies to the S.C. and the result is the sign, °, and ' occupied by the transiting Sun as shown in the ephemeris for that calendar year. The time of day the Sun reaches this ° and ' can then be calculated.

Wherever the Sun may be at any time of day on any day of the calendar year, change the algebraic sign before the S.C. and add it to the sign, °, and ' occupied at the time of day on that calendar date by the Sun, and the result is the sign, °, and ' occupied by the minor-progressed Moon on that calendar date.

Finding the Minor Progression Date

Each calendar year of 365.25 days is equivalent to 27.3 days of ephemeris time (minor progression time), which is the time it takes the minor-progressed Moon to complete the cycle though all the 12 zodiacal signs and return to the sign, °, and ' it occupied in the birth chart. The Minor Progression Date (abbreviated Mip. D.)—the ephemeris date on which the minor-progressed Moon again occupies the sign, °, and ' it occupied in the birth chart—for any calendar year may be found by counting ahead in the ephemeris as many returns of the Moon to the sign, °, and ' it occupies in the chart of birth as years of life have elapsed since birth.

Or, multiply the number of years that have elapsed since birth by 27.3. Then divide the product by 365 (number of days in a year) and call the quotient years. Divide the remaining days by 30 and call the quotient months. The number of years, months and days thus ascertained for each year after birth up to 96 years are given in the Minor Progression Date Table on pages 84 and 85. Then to the year, month and day of birth, add the years, months and days of the minor-progressed interval thus ascertained. This will give the approximate ephemeris date of the Mip. D. Move forward or backward in the ephemeris from this approximate Mip. D. until the ephemeris shows the Moon in the sign, °, and ' it occupies in the birth chart. This ephemeris day is the Minor Progression Date.

Finding the Minor Ephemeris Date

The Minor Ephemeris Date (abbreviated MED) is the date in the ephemeris from which the minor-progressed positions of the planets are calculated, or on which the minor-progressed planets make aspects to the birth chart or major-progressed positions.

Inspection of the ephemeris will show the MED on which the minor-progressed planets make aspects to birth-chart or major-progressed positions. To find the MED on which to calculate the minor-progressed positions of the planets for any calendar date, after changing the sign before the S.C., algebraically add it to the sign, °, and ' occupied by the transiting Sun on that calendar date at the time of day for which the minor-progressed positions are required. This gives the sign, °, and occupied by the minor-progressed Moon on that calendar date and at that time of day.

Then find the approximate Mip. D. for that calendar year. If the calendar date is before the birthday of that year, move back in the ephemeris from the approximate Mip. D. until the Moon is found in the indicated sign, °, and '. If the calendar date is after the birthday of that year, move ahead in the ephemeris from the approximate Mip. D. until the Moon is found in the indicated sign, °, and '. The ephemeris date so located is the MED.

Finding the Minor-Progressed Positions of the Planets on a Given Calendar Date

First find the sign, °, and ' occupied by the transiting Sun on the given calendar date, and for the precise time of day, just as it is found in erecting a birth chart for the day and time of day of birth. Then, as above explained, use the S.C. to find the precise sign, °, and ' occupied by the minor-progressed Moon for this calendar date and time of day. From this, as previously explained, find the MED for this calendar date.

Find (a) the daily motion of the planet in °s, and 's on the MED.

Find (c) the daily motion of the Moon in °s and 's on the MED.

Find (d) the °s and 's the sign, °, and ' occupied by the minor-progressed Moon on the calendar date and time of day, as above found, is from the sign, °, and ' occupied by the Moon on the MED.

By proportion, reduce (a), (c) and (d) to 's.

Multiply (d) by (a) and divide the product by (c). This gives (b), the distance in 's the planet is from its MED position.

By logarithms, add log. (a) to log. (d), and from the sum subtract log. (c). The result is log. (b), the °s and 's the planet has moved from its MED position.

If the position of the minor-progressed Moon for the given calendar date is less than its position on the MED and the planet is retrograde, add the °s and 's so found to its MED position. If the position of the minor-progressed Moon is less than its position on the MED and the planet is direct in motion, subtract the °s and 's so found from its MED position. If the position of the minor-progressed Moon is greater than its position on the MED and the planet is retrograde in motion, subtract the °s and 's so found from its MED position. If the position of the minor-progressed Moon is greater than its position on the MED and the planet is direct in motion, add the °s and 's so found to its MED position. This gives the minor-progressed position of the planet on the given calendar date.

For the minor-progressed declination of the planet, for (a) use its daily motion by declination, and find (b), the °s and 's it is by declination from its MED position just as the °s and 's from its zodiacal MED position were above found.

Example 1. For the chart 317b, given on page 86, calculate all the minor-progressed positions for January 19, 1932. The first step in all minor-progressed calculations is to find the Solar Constant. Subtracting the position of birth-chart Sun, 4S 12° 36', from the position of birth-chart Moon, 11S 22° 31', gives the Solar Constant as 7S 9° 55'.

The second step in finding minor-progressed positions is to find the position of minor-progressed Moon for the calendar date. Turning to January 19, 1932, in the ephemeris we find the transiting Sun at Greenwich noon 10S 28° 13'. Changing the algebraic sign before the S.C. we add its 7S 9° 55' to the transiting Sun, 10S 28° 13'. This gives the position of minor-progressed Moon as 6S 8° 08'.

The third step in finding minor-progressed positions is to find the approximate Minor Progression Date. 1932 is 12 years after birth. We look on the Minor Progression Date Table, page 84, and find for 12 years of age 00y 10m 28d. Adding this to date of birth, 1920y 7mo 4d, gives the approximate Mip. D. as June 2, 1921.

The fourth step in finding minor-progressed positions is to find the MED. As Jan. 19 is before the birthday in 1932, we move back in the ephemeris from the approximate Mip. D. until we find the Moon near 8 Virgo 08. The MED is thus May 15, 1921, which shows the Moon 5 Virgo 21 and moving (c) 13° 55'.

To reach 8 Virgo 08 it must move (d) 2° 47'.

The daily motion of the planet on May 15, 1921, is (a).

For use in proportion we reduce 13° 55', which gives (c) 835'.

For use in proportion we reduce 2° 47', which gives (d) 167'.

For use by logarithms they are not reduced.

The daily motion of the Sun on May 15, 1921, is (a) 58'. By proportion, multiplying (d) 167 by (a) 58 gives 9686. Dividing 9686 by (c) 835 gives (b) 12'.

By logarithms, adding log. (a) 1.3949 to log. (d) .9356 gives 2.3305. Subtracting log. (c) .2367 from 2.3305 gives 2.0938, which is the log. of (b) 12'. Adding the 12' found by either method to the position of the Sun in the ephemeris on May 15, 1921, gives the minor-progressed position of the Sun at Greenwich noon for calendar date Jan. 19 1932, as 24 Taurus 18.

The daily motion of Mercury on May 15, 1921, is (a) 2° 09'. By proportion, reducing the 2° 09' gives (a) 129'. Multiplying (d) 167 by (a) 129 gives 21543. Dividing 21543 by (c) 835 gives (b) 26'.

By logarithms, adding log. (a) 1.0478 to log (d) .9356 gives 1.9834. Subtracting log. (c) .2367 from 1.9834 gives 1.7467, which is the log. of (b) 26'. Adding the 26' found by either method to Mercury's position in the ephemeris on May 15, 1921, gives the minor-progressed position of Mercury at Greenwich noon on calendar date Jan. 19, 1932, as 00 Gemini 37.

The minor-progressed positions of the other planets are found in the same way by using their daily motion on May 15, 1921, as (a). Their minor-progressed positions for Greenwich noon will be found around the outside of the chart on page 86. The declinations are handled in the same way by using the daily motion by declination of the planet as (a)

Thus on May 15, 1921, the Moon is decreasing in declination (a), 4° 26'. By proportion, reducing 4° 26' gives (a) 266'. Multiplying (d) 167 by (a) 266 gives 44422. Dividing 44422 by (c) 835 gives (b) 53'.

By logarithms, adding log. (a) .7335 to log. (d) .9356 gives 1.6691. Subtracting log. (c) .2367 from 1.6691 gives 1.4324, which is the log. of (b) 53'. Subtracting (as declination is decreasing) the 53' found by either method from the Moon's declination in the ephemeris on May 15, 1921, gives the minor-progressed declination of the Moon at Greenwich noon on calendar date Jan. 19, 1932, as 4 N 51.

Example 2. For the chart 317b, find minor-progressed M.C. and Asc. for Jan. 19, 1932. The Midheaven Constant (M.C.C.) for this chart, found according to the method given in chapter 2 (Serial Lesson 111), is minus 2S 14° 50'. Therefore to find the minor-progressed M.C., as explained in chapter 2, change the algebraic sign of the M.C.C. and add its 2S 14° 50' to the minor-progressed position of the Sun as above found, 2S 24° 18'. This gives minor-progressed M.C. at Greenwich noon on Jan. 19, 1932, as 9 Leo 08. Using the method given in chapter 2, it is found that when 9 Leo 08 is on the M.C. in latitude 30N., 5 Scorpio 55 is on the Asc. Therefore, at Greenwich noon on calendar date Jan. 19, 1932, minor-progressed Asc. is 5 Scorpio 55'.

Finding the Calendar Date on Which a Minor-Progressed Aspect to a Birth-Chart or Major-Progressed Position is Perfect

Find the MED in the ephemeris nearest the ephemeris time the aspect is perfect.

If a major-progressed position is involved, find the major-progressed position for the calendar date represented by the MED. Find its major-progressed travel during the number of days represented by the movement of the minor-progressed Moon on the MED. This is from 12 to 15 days of calendar time, as indicated by the Moon during the MED moving from 12 to 15 degrees.

Find (a) the gain in °s and 's of the minor-progressed planet on the major-progressed planet during the calendar interval represented by the MED. If the aspect is to a birth-chart position, (a) is the daily travel of the minor-progressed planet on the MED.

Find (b) the °s and 's the aspect is from perfect on the calendar date represented by the MED.

Find (c) the °s and 's the Moon travels on the MED.

By proportion, reduce (a), (c) and (b) to 's. Multiply (c) by (b) and divide the product by (a). This gives (d), the distance in 's the minor-progressed Moon is from its position on the MED when the aspect is perfect.

By logarithms, add log. (b) to log. (c), and from the sum subtract log. (a). The result is log. (d), the °s and 's the minor-progressed Moon is from its position on the MED when the aspect is perfect.

From the sign, °, and ' thus occupied by the minor-progressed Moon when the aspect is perfect, use the S.C. to find the sign, °, and ' occupied by the transiting Sun on the calendar date the aspect is perfect. If it is desired to know the time of day the minor-progressed aspect is perfect on that calendar day, calculate the time of day in the manner explained in chapter 7 (Serial Lesson 116).

Example 3. For chart 317b, find during calendar year 1932 when minor-progressed Sun is sextile Venus p. The chart on page 86 shows the position of major-progressed Venus on Jan. 19, 1932, as 27 Cancer 07. Looking back in the ephemeris from the approximate Mip. D. for 1932 (June 2, 1921), we find the Sun on May 18 in 26 Taurus 59 and thus near sextile Venus p. On this MED the Moon is 16 Libra 29. Subtracting the S.C. 7S 9° 55' from 7S 16° 29' gives the transiting position of the Sun on the MED as 12S 6° 34'. Looking in the 1932 ephemeris we find the Sun 6 Pisces 42 on Feb. 26, 1932. Calculating major-progressed Venus according to the method given in chapter 2 (Serial Lesson 111), gives its position on Feb. 26, 1932, as 27 Cancer 15. During the 13 days, movement of the Moon on the MED, calculated by the method given in chapter 2, Venus moves 3'. Subtracting this 3' from the 58' the Sun moves on May 18, 1921, gives the gain (a) 55'.

May 18, 1921, the Sun lacks (b) 16' of sextile 27 Cancer 15.

May 18, 1921, the Moon moves (c) 13° 19'.

By proportion, reducing 13° 19' gives (c) 799'. Multiplying (c) 799 by (b) 16 gives 12784. Dividing 12784 by (a) 55 gives (d) 232' or 3° 52'.

By logarithms, adding log. (b) 1.9542 to log. (c) .2558 gives 2.2100. Subtracting log. (a) 1.4180 from 2.2100 gives .7920, which is the log. of (d) 3° 52'.

Adding the 3° 52' found by either method to the position of the Moon on May 18, 1921, gives the minor-progressed position of the Moon 20 Libra 21. From this 7S 20° 21' subtract the S.C. 7S 9° 55' and it gives the position of transiting Sun 10 Pisces 26. Turning to an ephemeris for the year 1932 we find the Sun 10 Pisces 43, less than 12 hours' movement from the required position, on March 1, 1932. Thus Sun *m* is sextile Venus *p* March 1, 1932.

Example 4. For chart 317b, find during the calendar year 1932 when minor-progressed Sun is sesquisquare birth-chart Mars. The chart on page 86 shows Mars *r* 27 Libra 50. For the sesquisquare the Sun *m* can move to 12 Gemini 50. Looking in the ephemeris from the approximate Mip. D. for 1932 (June 2, 1921), we find the Sun on June 3, 1921, in 12 Gemini 20. On this MED the Sun moves (a) 57'. It lacks (b) 30' of the aspect. The Moon moves daily (c) 13° 44'.

By proportion, reducing 13° 44' gives (c) 824'. Multiplying (c) 824 by (b) 30 gives 24720. Dividing 24720 by (a) 57 gives (d) 434' or 7° 14'.

By logarithms, adding log. (b) 1.6812 to log. (c) .2424 gives 1.9236. Subtracting log. (a) 1.4025 from 1.9236 gives .5211, which is the log. of (d) 7° 14'. Adding the 7° 14' found by either method to the position of the Moon June 3, 1921, gives the minor-progressed position of the Moon 13 Taurus 21. From this 2S 13° 21' subtract the S.C. 7S 9° 55' and it gives the position of transiting Sun as 7S 3° 26'. Turning to an ephemeris for 1932 we find the Sun 3 Libra 11, and thus less than 12 hours' movement from the required position on Sept. 26, 1932. Thus Sun *m* is sesquisquare Mars *r* Sept. 26, 1932.

Finding the Minor-Progressed M.C. on a Given Date

Instructions for this are given in chapter 2 (Serial Lesson 111).

Finding the Minor-Progressed Asc. on a Given Date

Instructions for this are given in chapter 2 (Serial Lesson 111).

Finding the Sign, °, and ' on the M.C. for a Given Asc.

Instructions for this are given in chapter 2 (Serial Lesson 111).

MINOR PROGRESSIONS OF SUN AND ANGLES 97

Finding the Calendar Date From the Minor-Progressed M.C.

Instructions for this are given in chapter 2 (Serial Lesson 111).

Finding the Zodiacal Motion of Minor-Progressed M.C. or Asc.

Instructions for this are given in chapter 2 (Serial Lesson 111).

Finding the Calendar Date on Which an Aspect From Minor-Progressed M.C. or Asc. to a Major-Progressed or Birth-Chart Position is Perfect

Find the MED in the ephemeris nearest the ephemeris time the aspect is perfect. Find the sign, °, and ' of minor-progressed M.C. or Asc. on the calendar date represented by this MED.

If a major-progressed position is involved, find its major-progressed position for the calendar date represented by the MED. Find its major-progressed travel during the number of days represented by the movement of minor-progressed Moon on the MED. This is from 12 to 15 days calendar time, as indicated by the Moon on the MED moving from 12 to 15 degrees.

Find (a) the gain in °s and 's of the minor-progressed M.C. or Asc. on the travel of the major-progressed position during the calendar interval represented by the MED. If the aspect is to a birth-chart position, (a) is the travel of minor-progressed M.C. or Asc. on the MED.

Find (b) the °s and 's the aspect is from perfect on the calendar date represented by the MED.

Find (c) the °s and 's the Moon travels on the MED.

Then proceed as if the aspect were being made by a minor-progressed planet as previously explained.

Example 5. For chart 317b, find during the calendar year 1932 when minor-progressed M.C. is sextile Mars p. The chart on page 86 shows major-progressed Mars on Jan. 19, 1932, in 2 Scorpio 23. To reach the sextile M.C. must be more than 2 Virgo 23. From 6S 2° 23' subtract the M.C.C. 2S 14° 50' and it gives Sun *m* as 17 Gemini 33. Looking ahead from the approximate Mip. D. (June 2, 1921) we find the Sun on June 8, 1921, in 17 Gemini 08. This is the MED. To this 3S 17° 08' add the M.C.C. 2S 14° 50' and it gives the position of M.C. *m* on the MED as 1 Virgo 58. On this MED the Moon is 18 Cancer 04. Subtracting the S.C. 7S 9° 55' from 4S 18° 04' gives the transiting position of the Sun on the MED as 9S 8° 09'. Looking in the 1932 ephemeris we find the Sun 8 Sagittarius 06 on Nov. 30, 1932.

Calculating major-progressed Mars according to the method given in chapter 2 (Serial Lesson 111) gives Mars *p* on Nov. 30, 1932, in 2 Scorpio 45. During the 15 days movement of the Moon on the MED, calculated according to the method given in chapter 2, Mars moves 1'. The M.C. moves the same distance as the Sun on the MED. On June 8, 1921, it moves 57'. Subtracting the 1' Mars moves from the 57' gives the gain as (a) 56'.

On the MED the M.C. lacks (b) 47' of sextile Mars *p*.

On the MED, June 8, 1921, Moon moves (c) 14° 49'.

By proportion, reducing 14° 49' gives (c) 889'. Multiplying (c) 889 by (b) 47 gives 41783. Dividing 41783 by (a) 56 gives 746' or 12° 26'.

By logarithms, adding log. (b) 1.4863 to log. (c) .2095 gives 1.6958. Subtracting log. (a) 1.4102 from 1.6958 gives .2856, which is the log. of (d) 12° 26'.

Adding the 12° 26' found by either method to the position of the Moon June 8, 1921, gives the minor-progressed position of the Moon 00 Leo 30. From this 5S 00° 30' subtract the S.C. 7S 9° 55' and it gives the position of transiting Sun 9S 20° 35'. Turning to an ephemeris for the year 1932 we find the Sun 20 Sagittarius 17, less than 12 hours' movement from the required position, Dec. 12, 1932. Thus minor-progressed M.C. is sextile Mars *p* Dec. 12, 1932.

Example 6. For chart 317b, find during the calendar year 1932 when minor-progressed Asc. is square Neptune *r*: In example 2 we found minor-progressed Asc. on January 19, 1932, in 5 Scorpio 55. To make the square of Neptune *r* it must reach 10 Scorpio 12. According to the method given in chapter 2 (Serial Lesson 111), when 10 Scorpio 12 is on the Asc. in latitude 30N., 14 Leo 08 is on the M.C. From 5S 14° 08' subtract the M.C.C. 2S 14° 50' and it gives the position of Sun *m* when the aspect is perfect as 2S 29° 18'. Looking back in the ephemeris from the approximate Mip. D. we find the Sun on May 21, 1921, in 29 Taurus 52. Thus May 21, 1921, is the MED.

On the MED the Sun moves (a) 58'.

On the MED Sun is (b) 34' past the aspect.

Previous day to MED, Moon moves 12° 54'.

By proportion, reducing 12° 54' gives (c) 774'. Multiplying (c) 774 by (b) 34 gives 26316. Dividing 26316 by (a) 58 gives (d) 454' or 7° 34'.

By logarithms, adding log. (b) 1.6269 to log. (c) .2696 gives 1.8965. Subtracting log. (a) 1.3949 from 1.8965 gives .5016, which is the log. of (d) 7° 34'.

MINOR PROGRESSIONS OF SUN AND ANGLES 99

Subtracting the 7° 34' found by either method from the position of the Moon on May 21, 1921, gives the minor-progressed position of the Moon 18 Scorpio 15. From this 8S 18° 15' subtract the S.C. 7S 9° 55' and it gives the position of transiting Sun 1S 8° 20'. Turning to an ephemeris for 1932 we find the Sun 8 Aries 35, less than 12 hours' movement from the required position, March 29, 1932. Thus minor-progressed Asc. is square Neptune r March 29, 1932.

Example 7. For chart 317b, find during the calendar year 1932 when minor-progressed Asc. is square Mercury p. The chart on page 86 shows Mercury p on Jan. 19, 1932, in 9 Leo 58R. To reach the square the Asc. must be less than 9 Scorpio 58. When 10 Scorpio 05 is on the Asc. in latitude 30N. the table of houses shows 14 Leo 00 on the M.C. Subtracting the M.C.C. 2S 14° 50' from 5S 14° 00' gives the position of minor-progressed Sun 2S 29° 10'. May 20, 1921, the ephemeris shows the Sun 28 Taurus 54. Thus May 20, 1921, is the MED.

To the position of the Sun on May 20, 1921, add the M.C.C. 2S 14° 50' and it gives the position of minor-progressed M.C. on the MED as 13 Leo 44. Calculated according to the method given in chapter 2 (Serial Lesson 111), when 13 Leo 44 is on the M.C. in latitude 30N. 9 Scorpio 51 is on the Asc. Therefore minor-progressed Asc. on the MED is 9 Scorpio 51.

The Moon on the MED is 12 Scorpio 55. From this subtract the S.C. 7S 9° 55' and it gives the position of transiting Sun 3 Aries 00. The 1932 ephemeris shows Sun in 2 Aries 39 March 23. This is the calendar date corresponding to the MED. Calculating major-progressed Mercury according to the method given in chapter 2, gives its position March 23, 1932, as 9 Leo 55R. The aspect is from perfect thus (b) 4'.

On the MED, May 20, 1921, the Sun moves 58', which is also the movement of minor-progressed M.C. While the M.C. moves 60' from 13 Leo 00 to 14 Leo 00 the Asc. in latitude 30N. moves 51', and while the M.C. moves 58' the Asc., calculated according to the method given in chapter 2, moves 49'. Thus the Asc. on the MED moves 49', and during the 13 days, movement of the Moon on the MED major-progressed Mercury, calculated according to the method given in chapter 2, moves 1'. As Asc. is direct in motion and major-progressed Mercury is retrograde, we add the 49' and the 1' which gives the gain (a) 50'.

On the MED the Moon moves (c) 12° 54'.

By proportion, reducing 12° 54' gives (c) 774'. Multiplying (c) 774 by (b) 4 gives 3096. Dividing 3096 by (a) 50 gives (d) 62' or 1° 02'.

By logarithms, adding log. (b) 2.5563 to log. (c) .2696 gives 2.8259. Subtracting log. (a) 1.4594 from 2.8259 gives 1.3665, which is the log. of (d) 1° 06'.

Adding the 1° 02' found by either method to the position of the Moon on May 20, 1921, gives the minor-progressed position of the Moon as 13 Scorpio 57. From this 8S 13° 57' subtract the S.C. 7S 9° 55' and it gives the position of transiting Sun as 1S 4° 02'. Turning to an ephemeris for the year 1932 we find the Sun in 3 Aries 39, less than 12 hours' movement from the required position, March 24, 1932. Thus minor-progressed Asc. is square Mercury p March 24, 1932.

Finding the Declination of Minor-Progressed M.C. or Asc. for a Given Calendar Date

From the sign, °, and ' on the minor-progressed M.C. or Asc. find the declination as if it were a birth-chart position, as explained on page 42 of chapter 3 (Serial Lesson 112).

Finding the Motion by Declination of Minor-Progressed M.C. or Asc.

Instructions for this are given in chapter 3 (Serial Lesson 112).

Finding the Calendar Date on Which a Major, Minor or Transit-Progressed Planet, Progressed M.C. or Progressed Asc. Reaches a Given Sign, °, and ' of the Zodiac, or Reaches a Given ° and ' of Declination

In this problem (b) is the °s and 's the planet, M.C. or Asc. must move from its Map. D., MED, or Transit Date position to reach the given ° and '. The problem is handled exactly as if the progressing planet, M.C. or Asc. was this number of °s and 's from making an aspect to a birth-chart position.

Finding the Calendar Date on Which the Minor-Progressed M.C. or Asc. Makes a Parallel Aspect With a Major-Progressed or Birth-Chart Position

Find the MED in the ephemeris nearest the ephemeris time the aspect is perfect. If a major-progressed position is involved, find the major-progressed declination for the calendar date represented by the MED. Find the major-progressed travel by declination during the number of days represented by the movement of the minor-progressed Moon on the MED. This is from 12 to 15 days of calendar time, as indicated by the Moon during the MED moving from 12 to 15 degrees.

Find the declination in °s and 's occupied by minor-progressed M.C. or Asc. on the calendar date represented by the MED. Find the minor-progressed travel by declination of the M.C. or Asc. during the MED.

MINOR PROGRESSIONS OF SUN AND ANGLES

Find (a) the gain in °s and 's of the minor-progressed M.C. or Asc. in declination on the major-progressed position's travel by declination during the calendar interval represented by the MED. If the aspect is to a birth-chart position, (a) is the travel in declination of minor-progressed M.C. or Asc. on the MED.

Find (b) the °s and 's the aspect is from perfect on the calendar date represented by the MED.

Find (c) the °s and 's the Moon travels on the MED.

Then proceed as if the aspect were being made by a minor-progressed planet as previously explained.

Example 8. For chart 317 b, find the calendar date in 1932 when minor-progressed Asc. is parallel Mercury *p*. Major-progressed Mercury, as shown on the Map. D. July 16, 1920, has declination 14 N 13 on Jan. 19, 1932, and is decreasing declination by 8' per year by major progression. The table on page 106 of chapter 6 (Serial Lesson 115) shows that to reach declination 14 S 11 the Asc. can be 8 Scorpio 00. A table of houses shows that when 11 Leo 00 is on the M.C. the Asc. in latitude 30N. is 7 Scorpio 31. Thus when the aspect is perfect approximately 11 Leo 30 will be on the M.C. Subtracting the M.C.C. 2S 14° 50' from 5S 11° 30' gives the approximate position of minor-progressed Sun 26 Leo 40. Moving back in the ephemeris from the approximate Mip. D. for 1932, June 2, 1921, we find the Sun on May 18, 1921, in 26 Taurus 59. Thus May 18, 1921, is the MED.

May 18, 1921, the Moon is 16 Libra 29. From 7S 16° 29' subtract the S.C. 7S 9° 55' and it gives the transiting position of the Sun on the MED 12S 06° 34'. Looking in the 1932 ephemeris we find the Sun in 6 Pisces 42 on Feb. 26. Calculating the declination of major-progressed Mercury by the method given in chapter 2 (Serial Lesson 111) gives its position on March 13, 1932, as 14 N 12. It moves less than 1' during the 14 days, movement of the Moon on the MED.

To the position of the Sun on the MED 2S 26° 59' add the M.C.C. 2S 14° 50' and it gives minor-progressed M.C. on the MED as 5S 11° 49'. Calculated by the method given in chapter 2 (Serial Lesson 111), when 11 Leo 49 is on the M.C. in latitude 30N. the Asc. is 8 Scorpio 30. This is its position on the MED. On the MED the Sun moves 58'. This is also the travel of the M.C. on the MED. Calculated according to the method given in chapter 2, while the M.C. moves 58' the Asc. moves 50'. The table on page 106 of chapter 6 (Serial Lesson 115) shows that when the Asc. in 8 Scorpio 00 moves 60' the declination moves 19'. Calculated by the method given in chapter 3 (Serial Lesson 112), 8 Scorpio 30 thus has declination 14 S 21. While the Asc. travels the 50' on the MED by zodiacal motion, calculated by the same method the

Asc. increases declination 16'. This is the travel by declination of minor-progressed Asc. on the MED. As Mercury does not change declination during the MED the gain is (a) 16'.

As minor-progressed Asc. on the MED is 14 S 21 increasing in declination, and major-progressed Mercury on the MED is 14 N 12, the aspect is from perfect (b) 9'.

On the MED between May 17 and May 18, 1921, the Moon is moving (c) 13° 31'.

By proportion, reducing 13° 31 ' gives (c) 811'. Multiplying (c) 811 by (b) 9 gives 7299. Dividing 7299 by (a) 16 gives 456' or 7° 36'.

By logarithms, adding log. (b) 2.2041 to log. (c) .2493 gives 2.4534. Subtracting log. (a) 1.9542 from 2.4534 gives .4992, which is the log. of 7° 36'.

Subtracting the 7° 36' found by either method from the position of the Moon May 18, 1921, gives the minor-progressed position of the Moon when the aspect is perfect as 8 Libra 53. From this 7S 8° 53' subtract the S.C. 7S 9° 55' and it gives the position of transiting Sun as 11S 28° 58'. Turning to an ephemeris for 1932, we find the Sun 11 Aquarius 38, less than 12 hours' movement from the required position, on Feb. 18, 1932. Thus Asc. *m* is parallel Mercury *p* Feb. 18, 1932.

Example 9. For chart 317b, find the calendar date in 1932 when minor-progressed M.C. is parallel Jupiter *p*. Major-progressed Jupiter, as shown by the Map. D. July 16, 1920, has declination 15 N 15 and decreasing 4' per year by major progression. When 18 Leo 00 is on the M.C. the declination of M.C. is 15 N 26, and decreasing 19' while M.C. moves 60'. When 18 Leo 30 is on M.C. minor-progressed Sun is 3 Gemini 40, which gives the MED May 25, 1921, with Sun 3 Gemini 43. May 25, 1932, the Moon is 15 Capricorn 23. Subtracting from this the S.C. gives calendar date for MED May 26, 1932. Major-progressed Jupiter on May 26, 1932, has declination 15 N 14 and moves less than 1' during the 12 days, interval of the MED.

minor-progressed M.C. on the MED is 18 Leo 33 with declination 15 N 16. The aspect is from perfect (b) 2'.

minor-progressed M.C. on the MED moves 58' by zodiacal motion and decreases declination 18'. As Jupiter does not change declination the gain is (a) 18'.

On the MED, May 25, 1921, the Moon is moving (c) 11° 59'.

Solving from this point on as if the aspect were being made by a minor-progressed planet we find minor-progressed M.C. parallel Jupiter p May 28, 1932.

∽

Chapter 6

Minor Progressions of Moon and Planets

Serial Lesson Number 115
Original Copyright, 1934
Elbert Benjamine
a.k.a. C. C. Zain

Copyright 2014, The Church of Light

TABLE OF HOUSE CUSP DECLINATIONS

♈	N	♍	♉	N	♌	♊	N	♋
♎	S	♓	♏	S	♒	♐	S	♑
Deg.	Dec.	Deg.	Deg.	Dec.	Deg.	Deg.	Dec.	Deg.
0	0:00		0	11:28		0	20:09	
1	0:23	29	1	11:49	29	1	20:22	29
2	0:47	28	2	12:11	28	2	20:34	28
3	1:12	27	3	12:31	27	3	20:46	27
4	1:36	26	4	12:52	26	4	20:57	26
5	1:59	25	5	13:12	25	5	21:08	25
6	2:23	24	6	13:32	24	6	21:18	24
7	2:47	23	7	13:52	23	7	21:29	23
8	3:11	22	8	14:11	22	8	21:39	22
9	3:34	21	9	14:30	21	9	21:48	21
10	3:58	20	10	14:49	20	10	21:57	20
11	4:22	19	11	15:07	19	11	22:06	19
12	4:45	18	12	15:26	18	12	22:14	18
13	5:08	17	13	15:45	17	13	22:22	17
14	5:32	16	14	16:03	16	14	22:30	16
15	5:55	15	15	16:20	15	15	22:36	15
16	6:18	14	16	16:38	14	16	22:42	14
17	6:41	13	17	16:55	13	17	22:49	13
18	7:04	12	18	17:12	12	18	22:54	12
19	7:27	11	19	17:29	11	19	23:00	11
20	7:49	10	20	17:45	10	20	23:04	10
21	8:11	9	21	18:01	9	21	23:08	9
22	8:34	8	22	18:16	8	22	23:12	8
23	8:56	7	23	18:32	7	23	23:16	7
24	9:19	6	24	18:47	6	24	23:19	6
25	9:41	5	25	19:01	5	25	23:22	5
26	10:02	4	26	19:16	4	26	23:23	4
27	10:25	3	27	19:30	3	27	23:24	3
28	10:46	2	28	19:44	2	28	23:25	2
29	11:07	1	29	19:57	1	29	23:26	1
	11:28	0		20:09	0		23:27	0

Computed by Dr. Harold E. Iden

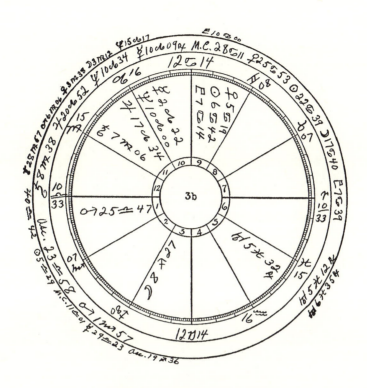

Minors: Birth Chart 3b

June 28, 1920, 12:23 p.m. CST. 89W. 40:40N.
L.D. March 22, 1920. M.C.C. minus 0S 5° 32'.
Solar Constant, minus 5S 1° 45'.

*Major progressions in outer circle for March 22, 1937.
Minor progressions outside chart for March 22, 1937.*

1924 Jan. 20, Venus *m* trine Uranus *r*.

1934 May 18, Sun *m* conjunction Sun *p*.

1935 Aug. 22, Mars *m* trine Moon *r*.

1936 Sept. 11, Uranus *m* opposition Saturn *r*.

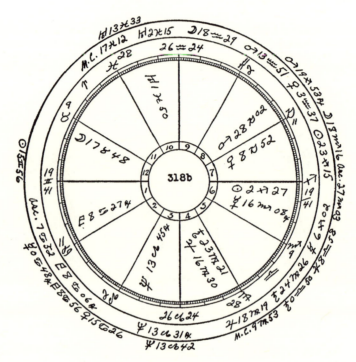

Minors: Birth Chart 318b

November 24, 1920, 6:00 p.m. CST. 95W. 39N.
L.D. May 24, 1941. M.C.C. minus 2S 23° 57'.
Solar Constant, plus 6S 14° 39'.

*Major progressions in outer circle for May 24, 1941.
Minor progressions outside chart for May 24, 1941.*

1933 June 1, Venus m parallel Saturn p.

1936 Sept. 11, Mercury m semisextile Venus p.

1937 Feb. 19, Sun m square Asc. r.

1938 July 1, Mercury m conjunction Uranus p.

Chapter 6

Minor Progressions of Moon and Planets

T IS MUCH easier to determine the periods during which, because a major aspect is reinforced and given great power by one or several minor-progressed aspects to its terminals, an event of importance will come into the life due to the psychokinetic power of the thought cells thus given new energy than it is to determine how favorable or unfavorable the event thus attracted will be. The harmony or discord of the minor-progressed aspect to the major-progressed terminal seems to have no influence on the harmony or discord of the major-progressed aspect. But it does markedly step up its power.

These reinforced peaks of power of a major-progressed aspect afford a fair estimate of the psychokinetic power of the thought cells at those times to exert more than normal pressure characteristic of the planets involved in the major-progressed aspect, on the thoughts, behavior and environment. But the harmony or discord which exerts pressure on the thoughts, behavior and environment cannot be estimated by the harmony or discord of the progressed aspect alone. The thought cells influenced by the progressed aspect have their birth-chart harmony or discord. This may be considered their life-time normal. An independent minor-progressed aspect may coincide with a minor disagreeable or favorable event deviating from the normal, but its relative effect on the period in which it occurs is but a slight deviation from the normal harmony or discord; a deviation to be measured by the relative harmony or discord of the planets involved.

The harmony or discord of a major-progressed aspect between two planets is also a deviation from the normal harmony or discord of the thought cells. The harmony or discord added to the thought cells by a progressed aspect alters their birth-chart harmony or discord by the number of harmodynes or discordynes added to their birth-chart harmodynes or discordynes.

If, as frequently happens, the major-progressed aspect is between two planets one of which at birth had many harmodynes and the other of which at birth had many discordynes, the average benefit or detriment of the event influenced by the aspect may very closely be indicated by the average harmony or discord of the aspect, yet at the same time some of the events, or the same events, may markedly be a detriment or loss to the department of life ruled by the discordant birth-chart planet. For instance, the death of a loved one may mean a grave personal loss, but may also bring a financial inheritance of much value. Or a harmonious marriage may bring estrangement of friends who oppose it.

Instances occur in which, because the birth-chart discord of the planets involved is so great, a progressed trine brings loss and grief into the life. And other instances occur in which, because the birth-chart harmony of the planets involved is so great, a progressed square or opposition brings good fortune into the life. Thus in estimating whether, and how much, a progressed aspect is favorable or unfavorable, the harmony or discord of each planet involved in the progressed aspect should be estimated. And if one of the planets involved has much harmony, the departments of life it rules are not apt to suffer much from any progressed aspect. But if the other planet involved has much discord, the departments of life it rules are apt to suffer severely from a heavy discordant progressed aspect, and are apt to benefit little from a heavy harmonious progressed aspect.

Both the average benefit or detriment to be expected from a progressed aspect, and the benefit or detriment to be expected from each department of life influenced, may be calculated quite precisely in terms of harmodynes and discordynes according to the rules given on page 200-202 chapter 7 (Serial Lesson 203), Course 16, *Stellar Healing*. But before this can be done, the birth-chart power and harmony of each of the two planets must be calculated, and the harmony or discord of the progressed aspect. These calculations are explained and examples given in Course 16, *Stellar Healing*. But whether the birth-chart harmony or discord of the planets involved in a progressed aspect are thus precisely calculated, or merely estimated by inspection, in appraising the fortune or misfortune of the event or conditions likely to be attracted by a progressed aspect the birth-chart harmony or discord of each planet involved in it always should be given due consideration.

What to Do Under Favorable Progressions Involving the Sun

Because the thought cells mapped by the Sun are so intimately associated with the nerve currents, the feeling corresponding to the favorable aspect involving the Sun should be held as consistently and strongly as possible, so that its harmonious energies, dominating the whole electromagnetic form, will find their way as Rallying Forces into other compartments of the astral body and thus benefit as many departments of life as possible.

One under such a progression should make an unusual effort to increase his importance and the scope of his influence. He will find that his Power to mold conditions is increased, and he should thus direct himself vigorously toward shaping various environmental factors more favorable to his ends. In this endeavor he will find those above him in position or influence more favorable

MINOR PROGRESSIONS OF MOON AND PLANETS

to his inclinations than usual; and he should make a special effort to form such contacts.

To women in particular the male sex will be more kindly disposed, and their help may be solicited. To them this aspect is favorable to making lasting attachments.

The Individual under a favorable progressed aspect involving the Sun will have at his command a vital reserve which if he persistently directs his mind and actions toward the accomplishment of something enables the thought cells to exert unusually strong psychokinetic power toward its realization.

It is, of course, more easy at such a time to accomplish those things indicated by the house positions of the Sun and the other planet involved in the aspect. Undirected, the thought cells will attract events belonging to the department of life thus indicated. But, because of their power as Rallying Forces, the Solar energies readily can be diverted into almost any other form of accomplishment.

To get the most out of such a Solar progression, therefore, the individual must know quite definitely what he desires to accomplish or attract. He must then keep this end steadily in mind and work persistently and with unfailing confidence to bring it to pass.

What to Do Under Favorable Progressions Involving the Moon

Although more receptive, and fluctuating more than those of the Sun, the thought cells mapped by the Moon also have an intimate association with the electromagnetic form and nerve currents. Energies coming in over the aerial to them thus readily become Rallying Forces to influence other departments of life, the thought cells governing which also are reached by some temporary stellar aerial.

But energies from the planets, either harmonious or discordant, become Rallying Forces only when the feelings respond to them. If we are to utilize favorable progressed aspects involving the Moon to the greatest extent, therefore, we must cultivate the ability to feel the harmony and exuberance they bring. If, instead, through habit or volition, we keep tuned in on some less pleasant vibration, the energies from the Moon will only be able to have a favorable influence through the activities of the thought cells they reach more directly.

The houses occupied by the Moon and the other planet involved in the aspect indicate the departments of life through which favorable conditions may be attracted with greatest facility. Contact with the public in general, efforts toward publicity, and Domestic affairs as a whole tend to flourish. To men in particular women will be kindly disposed and their help may be solicited.

At fairly frequent intervals throughout the life the Major-Progressed Moon makes favorable aspects to the birth-chart and major-progressed positions. There is thus opportunity present recurrently to tune in on planetary vibrations which may be made decidedly helpful. It will give exceptional power to these favorable vibrations if the person appraises their nature by taking into consideration the characteristic energy of the other planet involved in the aspect, and makes a persistent effort to keep his Mind and Feelings tuned to this rate of vibration. In this manner his nerve currents will pick up this harmonious energy in great volume, causing it for the time to become his dominant vibratory rate.

If people but understood the opportunities presented to them by even a favorable progressed aspect from the Moon, through affording them an easily accessible supply of harmonious energy to tune in on, it would open up possibilities for attainment of which they dare not dream at present.

What to Do Under Favorable Progressions Involving Mercury

Any progressed aspect involving Mercury gives additional energy to the thought cells which relate to the expression of conscious thought. That is, cerebral processes are stimulated into more than normal activity; and the trend of the thoughts so stimulated will be colored strongly by the characteristics of the planet with which Mercury is involved in the aspect. The things about which these thoughts chiefly revolve are those governed by the houses in which Mercury and the other planet involved in the aspect are located.

These conscious thoughts have the function of tuning the nervous system and the electrical energies that flow over the nerves in on inner-plane vibratory rates having a corresponding frequency and trend. In fact, it is through the thoughts and feelings which are deliberately cultivated that man has his greatest power to mold his own destiny. He can, through the proper selection of the subjects for his thinking, tune his whole electromagnetic form in on similar vibratory rates and pick them up, radio fashion, and thus saturate himself with energies of the desired quality.

These energies then act as Rallying Forces, and flow over all the temporary stellar aerials that may be present at the time in his astral body, adding their harmonious vibratory rates to the stellar cells relating to various departments of life. These cells thus gaining new energy, and feeling kindly disposed, then use their psychokinetic power to attract into the life fortunate events relating to their department. Thoughts and feelings are the implements by which character and destiny may be shaped to the desired ends.

Under a progressed aspect involving Mercury, however, unless the thoughts stimulated by the unusual access of energy to the stellar cells mapped by the terminals of the aspect are governed and steadied, they may give rise to nervous haste and flurry, to a condition of nervous tension, or to feelings that are not entirely harmonious and constructive in character. It is well, therefore, even under the most favorable aspect involving Mercury to keep the thinking directed calmly, steadily and harmoniously into some selected constructive channel. To do this, and to prevent scattering of the thoughts or the development of undue tensions, it may be necessary to spend effort in the cultivation of Power thoughts and Religious thoughts.

Favorable progressions involving Mercury give facility to, and success from, the expression of the thoughts. They are thus favorable to talking, drawing up written contracts, lecturing, teaching, writing, publishing, or the presentation to others of any product of thought, in whatever direction the talents lie.

What to Do Under Favorable Progressions Involving Venus

As the favors Venus brings are largely those that come through friendship and the kind offices of others, it is essential, if the most is to be made of a favorable progression involving Venus, that human contacts be afforded.

Venus is helpful to all types of artistic expression, to love making, and to affectional matters in general. These interests, therefore, may be cultivated at such a time if they seem desirable. But aside from these matters more obviously ruled by Venus, other interests which may be forwarded through friendship may be pushed.

Because Venus so seeks the line of least resistance the utmost in benefit is seldom obtained from her good progressions. The tendency is merely to have a happy time and to enjoy such pleasures as are offered by her bounty. But the kind wishes of others, their helpful suggestions, and their more material support, if proper initiative is taken, often can be made to lead toward some more important goal.

Excess in the pursuit of pleasure may develop even under a favorable progression involving Venus; but joy, buoyancy, and a happy outlook on life also are the qualities which under such a progression attract others to the person and cause them to favor him. Therefore, instead of shunning pleasure and the society of others, unusual effort should be made to mingle with people, to be congenial with them, and to conduce to their happiness and joy.

While the Safety thoughts are beneficial when there is an unfavorable progression involving Venus, the undue cultivation of them while under a favorable progression involving Venus dampens the exuberance and creates a chill which others feel. To attract the maximum benefit the Social thoughts of Venus must be permitted, and even encouraged, to express spontaneously. The effort to put everyone at his ease, to see that he is enjoying himself, taking delight in the companionship of others, and spreading the sunshine of happiness on every hand, afford the best opportunity for a favorable progression involving Venus to attract good fortune.

What to Do Under a Favorable Progression Involving Mars

Whatever Mars gains comes through the expenditure of energy, through unusual initiative, creative power, aggression and strife. We need not expect, therefore, that the conditions attracted by even a favorable aspect involving Mars will be free from antagonisms. Strife is usually unavoidable; but the favorable progression gives the additional energy and resources which enable gains to be made in spite of opposition.

For purchasing or handling machinery such an aspect is fortunate. Surgical operations submitted to then will be handled with unusual skill. Enemies will be more easily defeated. But even though the aspect is exceptionally harmonious it does not prevent the attraction of dangers. And there should be a deliberate attempt to avoid haste and impulse in both speech and action.

One thing, and one thing only, is needed under a favorable progression involving Mars. It is to direct all the energies, to the utmost extent, into constructive channels. This does not mean that the energies should be curbed, but they should be employed to build up, and not to tear down.

Through the exercise of initiative and energy one is able to forward his desires and ambitions, especially those indicated by the house positions of Mars and the other planet involved in the aspect. And following the exclusively constructive attitude, when antagonisms and strife develop, as they surely will, the least attention paid to them the better. Usually, if unnoticed, they shortly will subside.

If fighting is unavoidable, the chances too win are better than usual; but to the extent one can keep his energies fully directed toward the goal of some real accomplishment will satisfactory progress be made under a favorable aspect involving Mars. Under Mars inner-plane weather cultivate patience and take it easy.

What to Do Under Favorable Progressions Involving Jupiter

Jupiter is the most powerful influence to attract good fortune. This he does through abounding optimism and good fellowship, which others feel, and to which they respond by the desire to grant favors.

Jupiter is one of the Business planets, and his favorable progressions are advantageous to investments, merchandising and professional advancement. The influence is to attract patronage from those with ability to pay well. The contacts with others through clubs, societies, or the more direct avenue of salesmanship should be sought.

This is the progression under which selling can be done easiest and to best advantage. The raising of money is also not so difficult at this time.

As the helpfulness comes through others feeling good will and benevolence through their contact with the individual, proper contacts should be encouraged. In fact, no effort should be spared to come in touch with those who have it in their power to give assistance, and to create an atmosphere of hail-fellow, well-met on the occasion of such meetings.

What to Do Under Favorable Progressions Involving Saturn

The gains that can be made due to the influence of Saturn are brought by hard work, economy, organization, system, shrewd bargaining, shouldering responsibilities, and dogged perseverance.

By accepting work and responsibility that is attracted, through management and the performance of duties in a manner satisfactory to others, permanent advancement may be made under such a progression. Contacts with elderly people and those of a conservative turn, tend to bring opportunities for progress. This is the best of all progressed aspects under which to make purchases. One is attracted to those who are willing to sell at a low price.

Organization, reorganization, or cost-saving methods may be inaugurated in business, as Saturn is one of the Business planets. He is so negative, however, that even under his most favorable progressions the Power thoughts need some cultivation to give courage and vitality. And, to prevent the mind from dwelling too continuously on serious problems, social contacts and the encouragement of the Social thoughts are only less important than when there is an unfavorable progression involving Saturn. Under Saturn inner-plane weather keep your chin up and cultivate cheerfulness.

What to Do Under Favorable Progressions Involving Uranus

Mental pursuits, especially the study of astrology and occultism, are given a favorable impetus. Discovery, invention, the development of new ideas, and the handling of intricate machines and electrical devices also prove fortunate.

If so used it can be made the most powerful of all influences for intellectual, and perhaps even spiritual progress. The electromagnetic energies are strongly charged in a manner that enables the individual, through oratory or more intimate associations, to compel others to do as he desires. It tends toward sudden changes that prove fortunate; especially as opening new mental vistas.

Under such a progression some person often is attracted into the life, for a time to have a marked influence, but the attachment is seldom lasting. Nevertheless, through human contacts sudden and amazing opportunities may come. In fact, it is the sudden and unexpected which happens, and the individual should be prepared to take advantage of any circumstance which arises.

What to Do Under Favorable Progressions Involving Neptune

Such progressions favor outings and recreation, and are probably the best of all for investigating psychic phenomena and for the development of the psychic faculties. Projects of vast size may be presented, but they seldom yield more than a small part of the expected benefits.

It is a fine influence for bringing new ideals, which if found sound after the aspect has passed may be adopted as permanent aims in the life. All dramatic and artistic endeavors are favored, and inspiration from unseen sources is ready at hand. Imaginative works thus are executed with extraordinary facility.

All occult, mystical and astrological pursuits are encouraged. This is one of the best of all influences for true spiritual progress.

What to Do Under Favorable Progressions Involving Pluto

Under the influence of no other planet is it so easy to come in contact with intelligences of the unseen world, not through the psychic feeling and impressions encouraged by Neptune, but through direct interchange of thought.

This direct communion with those of the inner plane is not without its dangers. If the desires and thoughts are selfish, those thus tuned in on will be of similar disposition. The influence over the life of unseen entities, therefore, whoever they may pretend to be, needs critical examination.

Never, for a moment, should one surrender his power of discrimination, or permit control. After careful analysis, if information gained from such sources can be used for Universal Welfare, well and good. But Pluto has a subtle, inversive side which frequently convinces people they are being helpful to others when in reality they are limiting their expression and exercising undue restraint.

A favorable progression involving Pluto affords opportunity for group activity and cooperation; for joining with others to forward some worthy cause. Its finer side, which may be contacted under such a progression, is the most spiritual of all influences; and may thus be made to benefit others and yield the utmost to the individual in Spiritual Progress.

What to Do Under Favorable Progressions Involving the M.C.

A progressed aspect involving the M. C. forms a temporary stellar aerial between the dynamic stellar structure mapped by the planet and this broadcasting station. The chief energy picked up is that of the planet involved. Therefore use the instructions given under the heading what to do when this planet is under favorable progressions, and associate the thoughts there indicated as strongly and harmoniously as possible with thoughts relating to honor, business and publicity. And take pains to take advantage of all opportunities to forward these three matters, especially through the characteristics of the planet involved in the aspect and the house it occupies.

What to Do Under Favorable Progressions Involving the Asc.

A progressed aspect involving the Asc. forms a temporary stellar aerial between the dynamic stellar structure mapped by the planet and this ground wire. The chief energy picked up is that of the planet involved. Therefore use the instructions given under the heading what to do when this planet is under favorable progressions, and associate the thoughts there indicated as strongly and as harmoniously as possible with thoughts relating to health, the personality and personal affairs. And take pains to take advantage of all opportunities to forward these three matters, especially through the characteristics of the planet involved in the aspect and the house it occupies.

Using Favorable Progressions as Rallying Forces

Often there is both an unfavorable and a favorable progressed aspect within the one degree of effective orb at the same time. The more energy given the thought cells mapped by the unfavorable progressed aspect by thinking the type of thoughts characteristic of their planets and the nature of the aspect the more psychokinetic power they gain to bring unfavorable events into the life. And the more the individual associates closely with the environmental factors characteristic of the planets involved and the houses they rule the greater facilities are afforded this psychokinetic power to bring unfortunate events into the life.

To the extent the individual instead associates closely with the environmental factors characteristic of the planets at the same time involved in a favorable progressed aspect and the houses they rule will the thought cells they map have facilities for bringing into the life fortunate events. And by avoiding the environmental factors characteristic of the planets involved in the unfavorable progressed aspect and the houses they rule, there will be environmental resistance to whatever psychokinetic power they are able to use which will lessen the misfortune of the event they can attract.

And if the individual will keep tuned in by his thoughts and feelings on the harmonious vibrations characteristic of the planets involved in the favorable progressed aspect, not only will he supply their thought cells with additional energy which will increase their psychokinetic power to bring fortunate events into the life, but they will also act as Rallying Forces to give greater harmony to all the stellar cells reached by the aerials of all progressed aspects which at the time are within the one degree of effective orb.

When the individual's thoughts and feelings are tuned to a certain vibratory quality, the nerve currents, which are electrical energies, become conductors of this quality of astral energy and carry it readily to all the stellar aerials of the astral body. It is far easier to maintain the harmonious feeling characteristic of a planet while it is involved in a favorable progressed aspect than while it is involved in an unfavorable progressed aspect, or while not involved in a progressed aspect. And so long as this state of feeling is maintained the chief astral energy received by the stellar cells at the terminals of all the aerials is of this type. Thus not only the stellar cells at the terminals of the favorable progressed aspect receive additional harmonious energy, but the thought cells at the terminals of other stellar aerials, particularly those at the terminals of other progressed aspects, also receive this harmonious energy, which tends to give them more harmonious desires. And thus having their desires conditioned more harmoniously they will use such psychokinetic power as they possess to bring into the life events which are more favorable than had their desires not thus been influenced by harmonious Rallying Forces.

Keeping Track of Minor-Progressed and Transit-Progressed Positions

It is especially important to keep track of minor-progressed positions so it can be known in advance whenever a minor-progressed aspect heavier than from the Moon forms to one of the terminals affected by a major-progressed aspect that is at the time within the one effective degree of orb; for such events as the major-progressed aspect brings will occur on one of the peaks of power thus indicated. Thus special precautionary actions should be taken during each such reinforcement period.

The minor-progressed Moon on the Mip. D. reaches the same sign, °, and ' the Moon occupies in the birth chart. Therefore a good way to keep track of the minor-progressed positions is first to find the Mip. D. for the current calendar year and in the ephemeris mark it with the date of the calendar year. Then move back in the ephemeris to the position of the Moon on the Mip. D. of the previous calendar year, and ahead to the position of the Moon on the Mip. D. of the following year, and mark these days in the ephemeris with the dates of these calendar years.

As the Moon moves approximately 1° a day by minor progression, the relation of the number of degrees of the sign occupied by the minor-progressed Moon to the number of the day of the calendar month is approximately constant. The number of °s it is ahead or behind the number of the day of the month at birth is approximately the number of °s minor-progressed Moon is ahead or behind the number of the day of any month. This difference is called the Lunar Constant. Each full month after the birthday finds the minor-progressed Moon in a subsequent sign, but approximately the same degree as at birth. Thus by making allowance for the Lunar Constant, starting with the birthday of the calendar year and the minor-progressed Moon in the same sign and ° as at birth on the Mip. D. for that calendar year, when moving backward or forward in the ephemeris from the Mip. D., mere inspection will indicate the calendar date when any of the planets are close to making an aspect to a birth-chart or major-progressed terminal. Having thus located the approximate calendar date when the aspect will be present, this MED can then be used to calculate when the aspect is perfect, and if it reinforces an important major-progressed aspect, when it comes within, and when it leaves, the one degree of effective orb.

When the transit positions of the planets are close to an aspect with a birth-chart or major-progressed position can be ascertained merely by scanning the ephemeris for the given calendar year. But for the positions of the minor-progressed and transit-progressed M.C. and Asc. the M.C.C. should be used.

Change the sign before the M.C.C. and algebraically add it to the sign, °, and ' occupied by the progressed Sun. This gives the progressed M.C. As progressed M.C. moves the same distance as progressed Sun, mentally adding the movement of progressing Sun to the M.C. will indicate the MED or Transit Date on which the M.C. forms an aspect. At the same time scanning a table of houses for this progress of the M.C. will indicate the MED or Transit Date on which the Asc. forms a zodiacal aspect. And at the same time also scanning the Table of House Cusp Declinations on page 162 as progressed M.C. and Asc. move forward will indicate the MED or Transit Date on which the M.C. or Asc. forms a parallel aspect with a birth-chart or major-progressed position.

Calculating Aspects Made by Minor-Progressed Planets

In the following examples, and in those in chapter 5 (Serial Lesson 114), minor-progressed positions are calculated for Greenwich noon, and minor-progressed aspects are calculated to the nearest calendar day. But by calculating the precise ' of transiting Sun for the given time of day at the place where the individual now resides, or the time of day where the individual now resides when the transiting Sun reaches the precise ' it occupies when the aspect is perfect, minor-progressed positions and minor-progressed aspects can be ascertained with a precision of less than half an hour of calendar time. How thus to ascertain the position of the transiting Sun at a given time of day, and the time of day it reaches a given of zodiacal longitude, for any location is explained in chapter 7 (Serial Lesson 116).

When an ephemeris is not available for the calendar year for which minor progressions are to be calculated, to ascertain the position of the transiting Sun use an ephemeris for the same century (1900 was not a leap year), and use a year which is a multiple of 4 added to or subtracted from the given calendar year. Thus for the year 1980, subtract 32 years and use the same date in 1948. When not thus using the ephemeris for the given calendar year there will be a few 's error in the position of transiting Sun, but its position will be precise enough for practical purposes.

The rules for finding minor-progressed positions for any calendar date, and for finding the calendar date when any minor-progressed aspect is perfect, are given in chapter 5 (Serial Lesson 114).

Example 1. For chart 3b, given on page 163, calculate all the minor-progressed positions for March 22, 1937: The M.C.C., calculated according to the method given in chapter 2 (Serial Lesson 111), is minus 0S 5° 32'. Subtracting the position of the Sun, 4S 6° 42' from the position of the Moon, 9S 8° 27', gives the Solar Constant as minus 5S 1° 45'.

The ephemeris on March 22, 1937, shows the Sun 1 Aries 27. Changing the algebraic sign before the S.C. and adding its 5S 1° 45' to 1S 1° 27' gives the position of minor-progressed Moon as 3 Virgo 12.

As 1937 is 17 years after birth, consulting the Minor Progression Date Table on page 130 of chapter 5 (Serial Lesson 114), we add the 1y 3mo 9d there found to the birth date, 1920y 6mo 28d, and find the approximate Mip. D. is Oct. 7, 1921. As March 22 is before the birthday, we move back in the ephemeris to Sept. 29, 1921, where we find the Moon 8 Virgo 01. This is the MED.

8 Virgo 01 is past 3 Virgo 12 (d) 4° 49'.

Between Sept. 28 and Sept. 29, 1921, Moon moves (c) 14° 49'.

Between Sept. 28 and Sept. 29, 1921, Sun moves (a) 59'.

By logarithms, adding log. (a) 1.3875 to log. (d) .6975 gives 2.0850. Subtracting log. (c) .2095 from 2.0850 gives 1.8755, which is the log. of (b) 19' travel by the Sun. Using its daily motion between Sept. 28 and Sept. 29, 1921, as (a), the travel of each planet may thus be found. Subtracting this travel from its position on Sept. 29, 1921, gives its minor-progressed position for March 22, 1937.

The minor-progressed position of the Sun thus found is 5 Libra 29. Changing the algebraic sign before the M.C.C., add its OS 5° 32' to this position of the Sun and it gives minor-progressed M.C. as 11 Libra 01. Calculated by the method given in chapter 2 (Serial Lesson 111), when 11 Libra 01 is on the M.C. in latitude 40-40N. 19 Sagittarius 36 is on the Asc. This is the minor-progressed Asc. The minor-progressed zodiacal positions for March 22, 1937, are given around the outside of the chart on page 163. The positions by declination may be found in a similar manner.

Example 2. For chart 318b, given on page 164, calculate all the minor-progressed positions for May 24, 1941: The M.C.C., calculated according to the method given in chapter 2, is minus 2S 23° 57'. Subtracting the position of the Moon, 2S 17° 48' from the position of the Sun, 9S 2° 27', gives the Solar Constant as plus 6S 14° 39'.

The ephemeris on May 24, 1941, shows the Sun 2 Gemini 55. Changing the algebraic sign before the S.C. and subtracting its 6S 14° 39' from 3S 2° 55' gives the position of minor-progressed Moon as 18 Scorpio 16.

As 1941 is 21 years after birth, consulting the Minor Progression Date Table on page 130 of chapter 5 (Serial Lesson 114), we add the 1y 6mo 28d there found to the birth date, 1920y 11mo 24d, and find the approximate Mip. D. is June 22, 1922. As May 24 is before the birthday, we move back in the ephemeris to June 7, 1922, where we find the Moon 18 Scorpio 16. Not only is this the MED, but as the Moon in the ephemeris is the exact ° and ' of minor-progressed Moon on May 24, 1941, no calculations are required for the planets. Their minor-progressed positions are their positions given in the ephemeris on June 7, 1922.

The minor-progressed position of the Sun thus found is 15 Gemini 56. Changing the algebraic sign before the M.C.C., add its 2S 23° 57' to this position of the Sun and it gives the minor-progressed M.C. as 9 Virgo 53. Calculated by the method given in chapter 2 (Serial Lesson 111), when 9 Virgo 53 is on the M. C. in latitude 39N., 27 Scorpio 03 is on the Asc. This is the minor-progressed Asc. The minor-progressed zodiacal positions for May 24, 1941, are given around the outside of the chart on page 164. The positions by declination may be found in a similar manner.

Example 3. For chart 3b, given on page 163, find the calendar date when major-progressed Mercury inconjunct Uranus r is reinforced in 1924 by minor-progressed Venus trine Uranus r.

This major-progressed aspect is perfect Jan. 1, 1924. As 1924 is 4 years after birth, consulting the Minor Progression Date Table on page 130 of chapter 5 (Serial Lesson 114), we add the 0y 3mo 19d there found to the birth date, 1920y 6mo 28d, and find the approximate Mip. D. is Oct. 17, 1920.

As Jan. 1 is before the birthday, we move back in the ephemeris from Oct. 17, 1920, to the MED Oct. 4, 1920, where we find Venus 5 Scorpio 46, and thus (b) 14' past trine Uranus r. Venus is moving daily (a) 1° 14'. The Moon between Oct. 3 and Oct. 4, 1920, is moving (c) 14° 11'.

By proportion, reducing 1° 14' gives 74'. Reducing 14° 11' gives (c) 851'. Multiplying (c) 851 by (b) 14 gives 11914. Dividing 11914 by (a) 74 gives (d) 161', or 2° 41'.

By logarithms, adding log. (b) 2.0122 to log. (c) .2284 gives 2.2406. Subtracting log. (a) 1.2891 from 2.2406 gives .9515, which is the log. of (d) 2° 41'.

Subtracting the 2° 41' found by either method from the position of the Moon on Oct. 4, 1920, gives the minor-progressed position of the Moon as 1 Cancer 10. From this 4S 1° 10' subtract the S.C. 5S 1° 45' and it gives the position of transiting Sun 29 Capricorn 25. Turning to an ephemeris for the year 1924 we find the Sun 29 Capricorn 1°, less than 12 hours' movement from the required position, on Jan. 20, 1924. Thus Venus *m* is trine Uranus *r* Jan. 20, 1924.

Example 4. For chart 318b, given on page 164, find the calendar date when major-progressed Venus trine Saturn *p* is reinforced in 1933 by minor-progressed Venus parallel Saturn *p*:

This major-progressed aspect is perfect June 25, 1933. As 1933 is 13 years after birth, consulting the Minor Progression Date Table on page 130 of chapter 5 (Serial Lesson 114), we add the 0y 11mo 25d there found to the birth date, 1920y 11mo 24d, and find the approximate Mip. D. is Nov. 19, 1921.

On Dec. 7, 1920, the Map D. for May 24, 1933, Saturn has declination 4 N 12. As May 24 is before the birthday we move back in the ephemeris from Nov. 19, 1921, until on Nov. 1, 1921, we find Venus in declination 4 S 15. This is the MED. On this date the Moon is 27 Scorpio 42. To this 8S 27° 42' we add the S.C. found in example 2, 6S 14° 39' and it gives the position of transiting Sun on the MED as 12 Gemini 21. The ephemeris for 1933 shows the Sun on June 3 in 12 Gemini 26. Thus June 3, 1933, is the calendar date representing the MED. As major-progressed Saturn moves only 2' a year by declination during 1933, its position on June 3, 1933, remains 4 N 12.

Minor-progressed Venus on the MED., Nov. 1, 1921, is 4 S 15 increasing in declination, and is thus past the aspect (b) 3'.

Between Oct. 31 and Nov. 1, 1921, Venus moves by declination (a) 29'.

Between Oct. 31 and Nov. 1, 1921, Moon moves (c) 13° 34'.

By proportion, reducing 13° 34' gives (c) 814'. Multiplying (c) 814 by (b) 3' gives 2442. Dividing 2442 by (a) 29 gives (d) 84', or 1° 24'.

By logarithms, adding log. (b) 2.6812 to log. (c) .2477 gives 2.9289. Subtracting log. (a) 1.6969 from 2.9289 gives 1.2320, which is the log. of 1° 24'.

Subtracting the 1° 24' found by either method from the position of the Moon on Nov. 1, 1921, gives the position of minor-progressed Moon as 26 Scorpio 18. To this 8S 26° 18' add the S.C. 6S 14° 39' and it gives the position of transiting Sun 10 Gemini 57. Turning to an ephemeris for the year 1933 we find Sun 10 Gemini 31, less than 12 hours' movement from the required position, on June 1, 1933. Thus Venus m is parallel Saturn p June 1, 1933.

Example 5. For chart 318b, given on page 164, find the calendar date when major-progressed Mercury square Uranus p starts to be reinforced in 1938 by minor-progressed Sun trine Mercury p.

Major-progressed Mercury square Uranus p is perfect Aug. 29, 1938. As 1938 is 18 years after birth, consulting the Minor Progression Date Table on page 130 of chapter 5 (Serial Lesson 114), we add the 1y 4mo 6d there found to the birth date, 1920y 11mo 24d, and find the approximate Mip. D. is March 30, 1922.

The aspect is perfect when Mercury p is 2 Sagittarius 10. It commences to be reinforced by Sun m when Sun m is approximately one degree from this position in 1 Aries 10. Moving back in the ephemeris from March 30, 1922, we find on March 22, 1922 Sun in 1 Aries 05. This is the MED.

The Moon on March 22, 1922, is 25 Capricorn 20. To this 10S 25° 20' add the S.C. 6S 14° 39' and it gives the position of transiting Sun on the MED as 9 Leo 59. The ephemeris for 1938 shows the Sun on Aug. 2, 1938, in 9 Leo 31. Thus Aug. 2, 1938, is the calendar date representing the MED.

Calculating major-progressed Mercury, according to the method given in chapter 2 (Serial Lesson 111), gives its position on Aug. 2, 1938, as 2 Sagittarius 04. During the 12 days' movement of the Moon on the MED major-progressed Mercury moves 3'. As the Sun on March 22, 1922, moves 60', we subtract the 3' from the 60' which gives the gain (a) 57'.

minor-progressed Sun on calendar date Aug. 2, 1938, is 1 Aries 05 and major-progressed Mercury on calendar date Aug. 2, 1938, is 2 Sagittarius 04. Therefore Sun m is within the one degree of effective orb of trine Mercury p (b) 1'.

The Moon between March 21 and March 22, 1922, moves (c) 12° 11'.

By proportion, reducing the 12° 11' gives (c) 731'. Multiplying (c) 731 by (b) 1 gives 731. Dividing 731 by (a) 57 gives (d) 13'.

By logarithms, adding log. (b) 3.1584 to log. (c) .2945 gives 3.4529. Subtracting log. (a) 1.4025 from 3.4529 gives 2.0504, which is the log. of (d) 13'.

Subtracting the 13' found by either method from the position of the Moon on March 22, 1922, gives the minor-progressed position of the Moon 25 Capricorn 07. To this 10S 25° 07' add the S.C. 6S 14° 39' and it gives the position of transiting Sun 9 Leo 46. Turning to an ephemeris for the year 1938 we find the Sun 9 Leo 31, less than 12 hours' movement from the required position, on Aug. 2, 1938. Thus Sun *m* is applying trine Mercury *p* within one degree of orb Aug. 2, 1938.

Chapter 7

Transits, Revolutions and Cycles

Serial Lesson Number 116
Original Copyright, 1934
Elbert Benjamine
a.k.a. C. C. Zain

Copyright 2014, The Church of Light

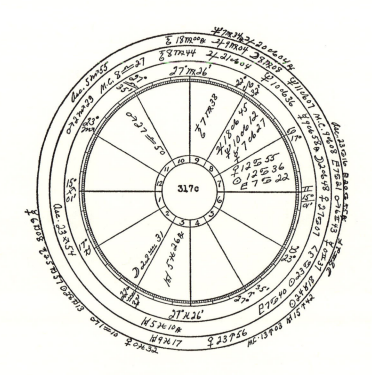

Transits: Birth Chart 317c

July 4, 1920, 5:00 p.m. CST. 90W. 30N.
L.D. Jan. 19, 1920. M.C.C. minus 2S 14° 50'.
Solar Constant, minus 7S 9° 55'.

Major progressions in first outer circle for Jan. 19, 1932.
Minor progressions in second outer circle for Jan. 19, 1932.
Transit progressions on outside for Jan. 19, 1932.

1932, Jan. 9, Mars t opposition Sun p.

1932, Feb. 7, Venus t trine Sun p.

1932, Feb. 15, Mars t conjunction Moon r.

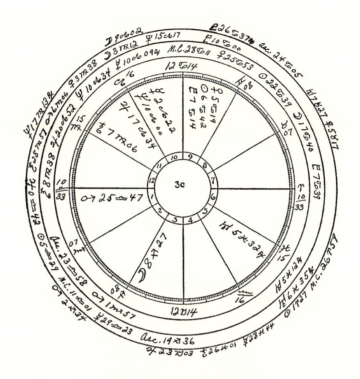

Transits: Birth Chart 3c

June 28, 1920, 12:23 p.m. CST. 89W. 40:40N.
L.D. March 22, 1920. M.C.C. minus 0S 5° 32'.
Solar Constant, minus 5S 1° 45'.

*Major progressions in first outer circle for March 22, 1937.
Minor progressions in second outer circle for March 22, 1937.
Transit progressions on outside for March 22, 1937.*

1937, July 2, Jupiter t square Asc. p.

1937, July 25, Sun t square Mars p.

1937, Aug. 6, Mercury t conjunction Saturn p.

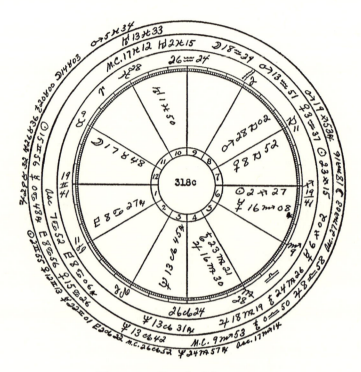

Transits: Birth Chart 318c

November 24, 1920, 6:00 P.M. CST. 90W. 39N.
L.D. May 24, 1920. M.C.C. minus 2S 23° 57'.
Solar Constant, plus 6S 14° 39'.

*Major progressions in first outer circle for May 24, 1941.
Minor progressions in second outer circle for May 24, 1941.
Transit progressions on outside for May 24, 1941*

1941, April 2, Saturn t square Neptune p.

1941, June 11, Mars t conjunction M.C. p.

1941, June 18, Uranus t trine Mars r.

Chapter 7

Transits, Revolutions and Cycles

HE most controversial of all astrological subjects relates to how much dependence can be placed on transit aspects. If an orb sufficiently wide is allowed, a transit aspect can be found that can be made to appear to account for every event of life. But when so wide an orb is used, some such transit aspect is present at all times, and there is nothing which clearly shows which of these numerous transit aspects indicates an event, and which does not. Under such circumstances the astrologer who has active extrasensory perception is able to pick the one which will coincide with an event. But those who rely exclusively on the aspect cannot do so; for while events do often coincide with transit aspects to birth-chart positions, innumerable transit aspects to birth-chart positions occur which do not coincide with any significant event.

The Church of Light has never maintained that transit aspects have no influence, but it has taught that their importance has been greatly over estimated by some. Furthermore, because statistical analysis of thousands of charts progressed to the time of an event indicates there is no need to consider them, the Hermetic System pays no attention whatever to the part of fortune, Moon's nodes, progressed minor house cusps, or the Arabic or so-called sensitive points.

Both in the birth chart and by progression it confines its attention exclusively to the positions of the ten planets, the midheaven and ascendant. For predicting by natal astrology the events probable in an individual's life it pays no attention to cycles or other such charts; having discarded their use after careful statistical analysis proved them often unreliable. It has found in addition to the birth chart the only reliable—and they are reliable—factors to be major progressions, minor progressions and transit progressions.

After a vast amount of statistical research on the matter we find the following rule fully justified:

RULE: Each reinforced Major-Progressed Constant of an event or disease is always released by a transit aspect heavier than from the Moon to one of its four terminals at the time the event occurs or the disease develops. And an independent minor-progressed aspect is always released by a transit aspect to one of the birth-chart or major-progressed terminals influenced by the minor-progressed aspect at the time the event takes place.

Thus even as minor-progressed aspects have two distinct influences, so also have transit-progressed aspects. They exert a power, and a harmony or discord 1/365.25 of the power and harmony or discord of the same aspect between the same two planets when made by major-progressed aspect. The psychokinetic power of the thought cells receiving new energy through transit-progressed aspects thus enables them to attract into the life inconsequential events. Inconsequential events coincide with characteristic transit-progressed aspects.

But in addition to this independent influence, if the transit-progressed aspect is to one of the terminals (as both birth-chart and progressed positions are terminals, unless a planet aspects its birth-chart place each progressed aspect has four terminals) of a major-progressed aspect, it has a trigger effect, tending to release either the minor-progressed aspect or the major-progressed aspect, or both.

If a match is lighted in a room filled with cooking gas, neither the power of the explosion nor the resulting destruction is commensurate with the limited energy of the match. The power was there, and the flame of the match merely released it. The power which projects a bullet from a gun does not lie in the trigger nor in the finger which presses it. The power is in the powder. That power is released when the trigger is pressed. Until the trigger is pressed the power is not released. And we have ample statistical data indicating that transit aspects have very little power in themselves, but that they exert a trigger effect which tends to release the power of reinforced major-progressed aspects, and also the power of independent minor-progressed aspects.

It will now be apparent why some think transits are so powerful. At the time they happen there is always a transit aspect within one degree of perfect involving the planets having an influence over important events. However, those who ignore major-progressed aspects, on an average miss one-half of such significant transit aspects; for the transit aspect to the major-progressed position of a planet is as powerful as the same transit aspect to the birth-chart position of the same planet. The main point, however, is that no transit aspect coincides with an important event in an individual's life unless at the SAME TIME there is a major-progressed aspect involving the aspected planet which is reinforced by a minor-progressed aspect.

To sum the whole matter up, nearly half a century of observation, and a quarter of a century of C. of L. statistical research, convinces us that for major events primary reliance should be placed only on the Major-Progressed Constants of the event. Minor events take place only during the periods indicated by minor-progressed aspects, and major events take place only during the peaks of power indicated by minor-progressed aspects which reinforce ALL the Major-Progressed Constants of the event. And the actual event takes place only when this reinforced power is released by the trigger effect of a transit aspect to one of the terminals of ALL the Major-Progressed Constants of the event.

Symbolically, the Sun is the father and the Moon is the mother, "Male and female created he them." In higher forms of life it requires the union of male and female to conceive offspring. The Hermetic Axiom, "As it is above, so it is below," is thus verified still further by finding that both Sun measured progressed aspects and Moon measured progressed aspects influencing ALL its Progressed Constants must join in the production of a major event.

In addition to gestation, however, before the event is born the energy must be released. It must become manifest on earth. As in human birth after gestation has been completed there must be the pains of labor or their equivalent before the child is released to take its own first independent breath, so in the delivery of any major event, after gestation due to major-progressed aspect and minor reinforcement progressed aspect, before the event is released in the physical world there must also be a transit aspect to the significant birth-chart or major-progressed terminal.

The above rule enables us to eliminate the possibility of a given event or the commencement of a given disease, even during those periods while the Major-Progressed Constants are within the one effective degree of orb, and all are being reinforced by minor-progressed aspects, except during those limited periods when ALL these Major-Progressed Constants are also being released by transit aspects.

It assists greatly in rectifying birth charts, as indicated on page 148 of chapter 8 (Serial Lesson 117), and it enables us more precisely to time indicated events; for the event will not only occur on one of the peaks of power indicated when ALL the Major-Progressed Constants are reinforced by minor-progressed aspects, but it will occur during one of these peaks of power ONLY at a time when there is also a transit aspect releasing ALL the reinforced Major-Progressed Constants of the event or disease.

But thus to be sure they are eliminated during a given period, and that a certain type of event will not occur because the trigger effect is absent, not only the zodiacal transit positions of the ten planets and the M.C. and the Asc. must be precisely ascertained, but the declinations also of all twelve transit positions. Such precision also on occasions may be required to be sure that the trigger effect is present at the time the effort is made to bring some favorable event to pass.

Transit-Progressed Aspects are of Value Only When Made to Birth-Chart Planets or to Major-Progressed Planets

Experience proves that the aspects among themselves of transit-progressed aspects—the aspects formed in the sky—afford so little energy that, while they should be considered in starting ventures or in doing some important thing, otherwise their influence should be neglected.

But as pointed out in chapter 1 (Serial Lesson 19), transit movements through the houses, especially the slower moving planets through angular houses, should be noted. And especially the conjunction with, or opposition to, birth-chart or major-progressed positions made by the slower moving planets should be noted, in addition to the trigger effect of transit aspects in releasing reinforced major-progressed aspects or in releasing minor-progressed aspects.

When we consider that the energy of a transit-progressed aspect is 1/365.25 that of the same major-progressed aspect, we are apt to jump to the conclusion that their influence is too small to be noticed. But the importance of an event attracted by psychokinetic power is not in direct proportion to the number of astrodynes of the planetary energy stimulating that power. When an individual has a number of major-progressed aspects involving the same planet, the accessory energy acquired by the thought cells mapped by that planet enables them to bring into the life an event more important than if there had been but one similar major-progressed aspect involving that planet. But if the energy thus received by the thought cells is five times that received under a single similar aspect, it does not indicate the event attracted will be five times as important. Experience indicates it is likely to be less than twice as important, and perhaps only one and one-half times as important.

Under ordinary circumstances the resistance of environment to an inconsequential event is so small that even 1/365.25 the power of a major-progressed aspect, such as that of a transit aspect, may be enough to bring it to pass. But commonly the resistance of environment to really important events is so great that a similar major-progressed aspect may be able to bring into the life an event only a few dozen times more important. And five or ten times the power of a single major-progressed aspect may be able to bring into the life, due to the resistance of environment to more important events, an event not more than twice as important as one due to a single similar progressed aspect.

Furthermore, the environmental conditions influenced by the inner-plane weather affecting the world, as indicated by the heavy aspects in the sky such as the oppositions and squares, and especially the conjunctions of the slower moving planets, and the inner-plane weather affecting nations, cities and groups of people as indicated by the major-progressed aspects in their charts of birth, have an important influence on the facilities for, or the resistance to, events indicated by progressed aspects in an individual's chart.

Our research department has observed that when drastic discords of some duration appear in the ephemeris, such as give a trend to world events of a disastrous nature, that the people through whom these world afflictions chiefly operate are those who have one or more of the planets involved prominent and severely unfavorable in their birth chart and by progression.

If the heavy aspects in the ephemeris are beneficial, those who have one or more of the planets involved prominent in their birth charts, and making favorable aspects by progression, are those most benefited.

The customary reaction of nations, cities, communities and other groups of people having a common governing authority is set forth in Course 13, *Mundane Astrology*. And the laws, customs, attitudes and fortune of the group to which an individual belongs must be taken into consideration as an environmental factor affording facility for, or resistance to, the psychokinetic power of the thought cells given energy by a progressed aspect to bring events into the life.

As a concrete example, during both World War I and World War II we had opportunity to observe the influence of progressed aspects in the charts of a great number of people who were called into service. For people within certain age limits, who were sufficiently sound of body and mind, almost any major-progressed aspect involving Mars took them into the armed service and thus changed the whole course of their lives. And under a progressed aspect involving Mars that under normal conditions would have attracted only a slight cut or burn, many a fine soldier was slain in battle.

Long Time Progressed Aspects

People get acclimated to either customary outer-plane weather or customary inner-plane weather. Major-progressed aspects between the slowly moving planets last for years, and may last throughout the whole life. The individual adjusts himself to this continuous inner-plane weather and considers it normal for his life. But at all times it is within one degree of effective orb the major-progressed aspect indicates the inner-plane weather is such that, given sufficient accessory energy from another major-progressed aspect, or sufficient reinforcement by a minor-progressed aspect to one or more of its terminals, at a time outer-plane environment offers facilities for such an event, it may enable the thought cells to attract into the life a characteristic event. Thus, because an aspect has been within the one degree of effective orb for years does not indicate that eventually it will not bring to pass an event typical of it, or that precautionary measures relative to it should be neglected.

While knowledge of the birth-chart and progressed aspects as set forth in this course is of tremendous value, it is obvious that the more precisely the psychokinetic power of the thought cells mapped by a planet is known, the better the individual knows the manner in which his thought cells will react; and the more precisely their harmony or discord is known, the better it is possible to estimate the amount and kind of precautionary actions needed to enable the individual to direct his life so that events and circumstances will be to his advantage. And to give this precision of information, the relative amount of psychokinetic power is measured in astrodynes, and the relative amount of harmony or discord, and thus the strength of their trend to bring harmonious conditions, or the strength of their trend to bring discordant conditions, into the life is measured in harmodynes or discordynes. How to compute as so many astrodynes, the POWER of any planet, aspect, sign or house in the progressed chart; and how to compute as harmodynes or discordynes the HARMONY or DISCORD of any planet, aspect, sign or house in the birth chart, or the HARMONY or DISCORD of any planet, aspect, combination of aspects, sign or house of the progressed chart, are explained with examples in Course 16, *Stellar Healing,* and are explained in greater detail in the reference book, *The Astrodyne Manual.*

What Not to Tell the Client

The object of the astrologer should be, not merely to demonstrate to his client and to the world at large how accurate in every detail his predictions are, but to be of as great assistance as possible to his client and to society as a whole.

He should never forget, therefore, that people react markedly to suggestion. In fact, a positive statement made by a determined mind builds a thought form in the astral which works from the inner plane to make the statement a reality. This power of suggestion, consequently, and the will of the astrologer to bring constructive events to pass, may be made of great benefit. On the other hand, it may be made a force of great destructive power.

The astrologer who predicts the death of an individual at a certain time, if the individual is aware of the prediction, may through suggestion contribute to the death. And even when the individual is unaware of the prediction, the thought form started by the astrologer, and added to by others who believe the astrologer's prediction will be fulfilled, may be an active agent toward causing tragedy.

Frightening people is iniquitous, because their fear attracts to them disasters that otherwise never would befall.

I do not believe the astrologer ever is justified in lying to his client; but it is within his professional jurisdiction how much of what he discerns he will tell. And in what he does tell his client, he has the opportunity, and should use it, to impart advice and information in such a manner that the suggestive power, and the thought power, of his words shall be constructive and of assistance.

The psychological effect of delineations and predictions should always be well weighed in connection with the temperament and probable reaction of those to whom made, before they are given.

Finding the Transit-Progressed Positions of the Planets on a Given Calendar Date

The transit-progressed positions of the planets for any time of day, on any calendar day, are found by calculating them exactly as if they were to be placed in a birth chart for that time of day on the indicated calendar day.

Find (a) the daily motion of the planet on the given calendar day.

Find (d) the minus or plus EGMT Interval from noon on the given calendar date.

(c) is 24 hours, or 1440 minutes.

By proportion, multiply (a) by (d) and divide the product by (c). This gives (b) the distance the planet travels during the EGMT Interval.

By logarithms, add log. (a) to log. (d). The result is log. (b), the distance the planet travels during the EGMT Interval.

(b) added to, or subtracted from, the Greenwich noon position of the planet on the calendar date gives the sign, °, and ' it occupies at the indicated time on the given calendar day.

Finding the Calendar Date on Which a Transit-Progressed Aspect to a Birth-Chart or Major-Progressed Position is Perfect

Find the date in the ephemeris for the calendar year nearest which the aspect is perfect.

If a major-progressed position is involved, find its major-progressed position for this calendar date. Find its major-progressed travel during 24 hours by dividing its travel on the Map. D. by 365. This travel is less than 1' for all the major-progressed planets other than the Moon.

Find (a) the gain in °s and 's of the transit-progressed planet on the major-progressed position during 24 hours. If the aspect is to a birth-chart position, or to any progressed planet other than the Moon, (a) is the daily travel of the transit-progressed planet. Major-progressed Moon moves 2' during 24 hours.

Find (b) the °s and 's the aspect is from perfect at the time of day represented by the ephemeris position of the transit-progressed planet.

(c) is 24 hours, or 1440 minutes.

By proportion, multiply (b) by (c) and divide the product by (a). The result is (d).

By logarithms, subtract log. (a) from log. (b). The result is the log. of (d). (d) found by either method is the EGMT Interval required for the planet to move from its ephemeris position to the perfect aspect.

If the aspect is formed before the positions given on the calendar date in the ephemeris, (d) is a minus EGMT Interval on that calendar day. If the aspect is formed after the positions given on the calendar date in the ephemeris, (d) is a plus EGMT Interval on that calendar day. From this EGMT Interval find the Standard Time (watch time), or the Local Mean Time, the aspect is perfect at the place where the individual resides thus:

Finding the Standard Time or the Local Mean Time for a Given Place From the Minus or Plus EGMT Interval From Noon

From the EGMT Interval find the EGM Time by subtracting a minus EGMT Interval from noon, or adding a plus EGMT Interval to noon.

If the place is east of Greenwich, to find the Standard Time add the number of hours of the Standard Time Zone of the place to the EGM Time; but if the place is west of Greenwich, subtract the number of hours of its Standard Time Zone from the EGM Time. The result is the sought Standard Time (watch time).

To find the Local Mean Time, multiply the number of degrees of terrestrial longitude the place is from Greenwich by 4 and call the product minutes of time, and multiply the additional number of minutes of terrestrial longitude by 4 and call the product seconds of time. This gives the time difference from Greenwich. If the place is east of Greenwich, to find the Local Mean Time, add the time difference to the EGM Time; but if the place is west of Greenwich, subtract the time difference from the EGM Time. The result is the sought Local Mean Time.

Finding the Transit-Progressed M.C. on a Given Date

Instructions for this are given in chapter 2 (Serial Lesson 111).

Finding the Transit-Progressed Asc. on a Given Date

Instructions for this are given in chapter 2 (Serial Lesson 111).

Finding the Calendar Date From the Transit-Progressed M.C.

Instructions for this are given in chapter 2 (Serial Lesson 111).

Finding the Zodiacal Motion of Transit-Progressed M.C. or Asc.

Instructions for this are given in chapter 2 (Serial Lesson 111).

Finding the Calendar Date on Which an Aspect From Transit-Progressed M.C. or Asc. to a Major-Progressed or Birth-Chart Position is Perfect

Find the calendar date in the ephemeris nearest the ephemeris time the aspect is perfect.

If a major-progressed position is involved, find its major-progressed position for the calendar date. As the major-progressed travel is less than 1' for 24 hours for all major-progressed aspects other than the Moon, except for the Moon, it may be ignored.

Find (a) the gain in °s and 's of the transit-progressed M.C. or Asc. on the major-progressed position during 24 hours. If the aspect is to a birth-chart position, or to any planet other than the Moon, (a) is the daily travel of the transit M.C. or Asc. Major-progressed Moon moves 2' during 24 hours.

Find (b) the °s and 's the aspect is from perfect at the time of day represented by the ephemeris position of the planet on the given calendar date.

(c) is 24 hours, or 1440 minutes.

By proportion, reducing (b) to 's, multiply (b) by (c) and divide the product by (a). The result is (d).

By logarithms, subtract log. (a) from log. (b). The result is the log. of (d).

(d) found by either method is the EGMT Interval required for the aspect to become perfect.

If the aspect is formed before the positions given on the calendar date in the ephemeris, this is a minus EGMT Interval on that calendar day. If the aspect is formed after the positions given on the calendar date in the ephemeris, this is a plus EGMT Interval on that calendar day. From the EGMT Interval find the

Standard Time (watch time), or the Local Mean Time the aspect is perfect at the place the individual resides according to instructions previously given.

Finding the Declination of Transit-Progressed M.C. or Asc. for a Given Calendar Date

From the sign, °, and ' of the transit-progressed M.C. or Asc. find the declination as if it were a birth-chart position, as explained on page 42 of chapter 3 (Serial Lesson 112).

Finding the Motion by Declination of Transit-Progressed M.C. or Asc.

Instructions for this are given in chapter 3.

Finding the Calendar Date on Which the Transit-Progressed M.C. or Asc. Makes a Parallel Aspect With a Major-Progressed or Birth-Chart Position

Find the calendar date in the ephemeris nearest the ephemeris time the aspect is perfect. If a major-progressed position is involved, find its major-progressed declination on the calendar date. As the major-progressed travel by declination is less than 1' during 24 hours, it may be ignored.

(a) is the daily motion in 's of the transit-progressed M.C. or Asc. by declination.

Find (b) the 's the aspect is from perfect at the time of day represented by the ephemeris positions of the planets on the calendar date.

(c) is 24 hours, or 1440 minutes.

By proportion, multiply (b) by (c) and divide the product by (a). The result is (d).

By logarithms, subtract log. (a) from log. (b). The result is log. (d).

(d) found by either method is the EGMT Interval required for the aspect to become perfect.

If the aspect is formed before the positions given on the calendar date in the ephemeris, this is a minus EGMT Interval on that calendar day. If the aspect is formed after the positions given on the calendar date in the ephemeris, this is a plus EGMT Interval on that calendar day. From the EGMT Interval find the Standard Time (watch time), or the Local Mean Time, the aspect is perfect at the place where the individual resides according to instructions previously given.

TRANSITS, REVOLUTIONS AND CYCLES 139

Finding the Time of Day an Aspect in the Sky is Perfect or a Planet in the Sky Reaches a Given Sign, °, and ' of Zodiacal Longitude or a Given ° and ' of Declination

It often is desirable to find when an aspect in the sky in perfect. In mundane astrology it is essential to determine the time of day of the New Moon, and the time of day each of the other planets passes from south to north declination. In weather predicting by astrology it is necessary to know the time of day when the Sun enters each cardinal sign, and the time of day Mercury enters each sign. In the problem as here solved it is assumed the motion of the planet is uniform. When, as often is the case of the Moon, and not infrequently in the case of Mercury, the motion is ununiform, this acceleration or deceleration must be taken into account if great precision is required. How to do this is explained later. But considering the motion uniform, in each of the mentioned problems:

Find the calendar date in the ephemeris nearest the ephemeris time the aspect or position is perfect:

Find (a) the daily gain in °s and 's of the faster moving planet on the slower moving planet either in zodiacal motion or by declination. If the planet is moving to a fixed position, such as 0° N 0' declination, (a) is the daily motion of the planet.

Find (b) the °s and 's the aspect is from perfect on the ephemeris date, or how far the planet must move to reach the fixed position.

(c) is 24 hours, or 1440 minutes.

By proportion, reduce (a) and (b) to 's. Multiply (b) by (c) and divide the product by (a). The result is (d).

By logarithms, subtract log. (a) from log. (b). The result is log. (d).

(d) found by either method is the EGMT Interval required for the aspect to become perfect or the required position to be reached.

If the aspect is formed, or the fixed position reached, before the positions given on the calendar date in the ephemeris, (d) is a minus EGMT Interval on that calendar day. If the aspect is formed, or the fixed position reached, after the position given on the calendar date in the ephemeris, (d) is a plus EGMT Interval on that calendar day. From the EGMT Interval find the Standard Time (watch time), or the Local Mean Time, the aspect is perfect or the fixed position is reached, at the place for which it is desired to erect the chart or know the time.

Example 1. For chart 317c, given on page 126, calculate all the transit-progressed positions for Jan. 19, 1932, at Greenwich Noon: The positions of all the planets are merely copied from the ephemeris for Jan. 19, 1932. Subtracting the birth-chart position of the Sun, 4S 12° 36', from the birth-chart position of the M.C., 6S 27° 26', gives the M.C.C. minus 2S 14° 50'. Changing the algebraic sign before the M.C.C. add its 2S 14° 50' to the position of transiting Sun on Jan. 19, 1932, 10S 28° 13', and it gives the transiting M.C. as 13 Aries 03. When 13 Aries 03 is on the M.C. in latitude 30, calculated by the method given in chapter 2 (Serial Lesson 111), 23 Cancer 16 is on the Asc. This is the transiting Asc.

Using the Table of House Cusp Declinations given on page 106 of chapter 6 (Serial Lesson 115), and the method given on page 42 of chapter 3 (Serial Lesson 112), we find that when M.C. is 13 Aries 03 it has declination 5 N 09, and that when the Asc. is 23 Cancer 16, it has declination 21 N 26.

Example 2. In chapter 5 (Serial Lesson 114) it was found for chart 317b that minor-progressed Sun was sextile major-progressed Venus on March 1, 1932, when transiting Sun was 10 Pisces 26. At what Standard Time of day at New York was this aspect perfect?

Turning to an ephemeris for 1932, on March 1 we find the Sun in 10 Pisces 43, and thus past the required position (b) 17'.

Between Feb. 29 and March 1, 1932, the Sun is moving (a) 60'.

(c) is 24h, or 1440m.

By proportion, multiplying (b) 17 by (c) 1440 gives 24480. Dividing 24480 by (a) 60 gives 408m, or 6h 48m.

By logarithms, subtracting log. (a) 1.3802 from log. (b) 1.9279 gives .5477, which is the log. of 6h 48m.

Subtracting the 6h 48m found by either method from Greenwich noon gives 5:12 A.M. As New York is Eastern Standard Time zone, 5h West, we subtract 5h from 5:12 A.M. and it gives minor-progressed Sun sextile major-progressed Venus, March 1, 1932, 12:12 A.M. New York watch time.

Example 3. In chapter 5 (Serial Lesson 114) it was found for chart 317b that minor-progressed Asc. was parallel major-progressed Mercury on Feb. 18, 1932, when transiting Sun was 28 Aquarius 58. At what Standard Time of day at Los Angeles was this aspect perfect?

Turning to the ephemeris for 1932, on Feb. 18 we find the Sun 28 Aquarius 38, and thus lacking from the required position (b) 20'.

On Feb. 18, 1932, the Sun is moving (a) 60'.

(c) is 24h, or 1440m.

By proportion, multiplying (b) 20 by (c) 24h gives 480. Dividing 480 by (a) 60 gives 8h.

By logarithms, subtracting log. (a) 1.3802 from log. (b) 1.8573 gives .4771, which is the log. of 8h.

Adding the 8h found by either method to Greenwich noon gives 8:00 P.M. As Los Angeles is in Pacific Standard Time zone, 8h West, we subtract the 8h from 8:00 P.M. and it gives minor-progressed Asc. parallel major-progressed Mercury Feb. 18, 1932, noon, Los Angeles watch time.

Example 4. When, by Local Mean Time at Chicago, Ill., did Mercury in March, 1932, enter the sign Aries? The ephemeris on March 9, 1932, shows Mercury 29 Pisces 21, and thus lacking from the required position (b) 39'.

On March 9, 1932, Mercury is moving (a) 1° 54', or 114'.

(c) is 24h, or 1440m.

By proportion, multiplying (b) 39 by (c) 1440 gives 56160. Dividing 56160 by (a) 114 gives 493', or 8h 13m.

By logarithms, subtracting log. (a) 1.1015 from log. (b) 1.5673 gives .4658, which is the log. of 8h 13m.

Adding the 8h 13m found by either method to Greenwich noon gives 8:13 P.M. As Chicago is 87:39W. we multiply the 87 by 4 and it gives 348m, and we multiply the 39 by 4 and it gives 156s, or 2m 36s. Adding these two sums gives 350m 36s West, or 5h 50m 36s West. Subtracting the 5h 50m 36s from 8h 13m 00s P.M. gives Mercury 00 Aries 00 March 9, 1932, 2h 22m 24s P.M. LMT., Chicago, Ill.

Example 5. At what Greenwich time of day on March 11, 1920, did Mars make the square of Jupiter in the sky? The ephemeris on March 10 1920, shows Jupiter *r* 9 Leo 03, and Mars direct 8 Scorpio 58. The aspect thus lacks of being perfect (b) 5'.

Jupiter is moving daily 5', and Mars is moving daily 3'. As one is direct and the other retrograde, we add the 5 and the 3, which gives the daily gain (a) 8'.

By proportion, multiplying (b) 5 by (c) 1440 gives 7200. Dividing 7200 by (a) 8 gives 900m, or 15h.

By logarithms, subtracting log. (a) 2.2553 from log. (b) 2.4594 gives .2041, which is the log. of 15h.

Adding the 15h found by either method to March 10, noon, gives Mars square Jupiter in the sky March 11, 3:00 A.M. Greenwich. With the planetary positions given to the 's position it works out 3:10 A.M.

Finding the Transit-Progressed Position of a Planet Uniform in Motion For a Given Time of Day

First find the increment or decrement of the planet during the 24 hours within which its position is to be found. The increment or decrement found by taking the difference in the planet's daily motion on two consecutive days is that of the planet's average travel. And this average travel is its precise travel midway between the two noons of each day. Thus starting at midnight with the average increment or decrement, the acceleration increases or decreases as the time is distant from midnight. Therefore, by proportion or logarithms find the increment or decrement at the midway point between noon and the time for which the position is to be calculated. Add the increment thus found, or subtract the decrement thus found, to or from the daily motion of the planet. Then use this as the average gain (a) and solve the problem in the ordinary way.

Example 6. For chart 318c, calculate the precise occupied by the Moon, making due allowance for acceleration. On Nov. 24, 1920, the Moon's position is 10 Taurus 36, while on Nov. 23 its position is 26 Aries 30. Its daily motion between these two days is 14° 06'. Its daily motion between Nov. 24 and Nov. 25, however, is 14° 30'. The amount of increment during 24 hours is thus 24'. The 14° 30' is the rate of its travel Nov. 24 at plus 12h Greenwich.

We desire the position of the Moon for plus 12h EGMT Interval. The position given in the ephemeris for noon is 10 Taurus 36. We want its increment at the midway point between noon and plus 12h, or at plus 6h. Plus 6h after noon is 18h after Nov. 23 at plus 12h, or it is 6h before Nov. 24 at plus 12h. The daily increment difference between the Moon's travel on Nov. 23 and Nov. 24 is (a) 24'.

(c) is 24h, or 1440m.

(d) is 6h, or 360m.

By proportion, multiplying (a) by (d) 360 gives 8640. Dividing 8640 by (c) 1440 gives (b) 6'. By logarithms, adding log. (a) 1.7781 to log. (d) .6021 gives 2.3802, which is the log. of (b) 6'.

TRANSITS, REVOLUTIONS AND CYCLES 143

Subtracting the 6' increment found by either method from the 14° 30' travel of the Moon on Nov. 24 at plus 12h, gives the average travel at midway point between noon and plus 12h as 14° 24'.

Without allowing for acceleration and calculating in the ordinary manner (a) is 14° 30'. Using this daily motion gives the Moon's position as 17 Taurus 51. But allowing for acceleration (a) is 14° 24'. This gives the position of the Moon more precisely as 17 Taurus 48, which is the position given it in charts 318, 318b and 318c.

Finding the Time of Day a Transit-Progressed Planet Uniform in Motion Reaches a Given Position

First find the increment or decrement of the planet during the 24 hours within which the time of its position is to be found. The increment or decrement found by taking the difference in the planet's daily motion on two consecutive days is that of the planet's average travel. And this average travel is its precise travel midway between the two noons of each day. Thus starting at midnight with the average increment or decrement, the acceleration increases or decreases as the planet is distant from midnight. Therefore, by proportion or logarithms find the increment or decrement at the midway point between the planet's position at noon and the given position. Add the increment thus found, or subtract the decrement thus found, to or from the daily motion of the planet. Then use this as the average gain (a) and solve the problem in the ordinary way.

Example 7. When, in March, 1920, making due allowance for acceleration, does the Moon enter the sign Aquarius? On March 14, 1920, the position of the Moon is 12 Capricorn 44, and on March 15 it is 24 Capricorn 53. Its daily motion is thus 12° 09'. Its daily motion between March 15 and March 16 is 12° 24'. The amount of increment during 24h is thus 15'.

The increment on March 15 at noon is ½ of 15 or 8'. The motion at noon, therefore, is 8' less than the 12° 24' daily motion, or 12° 16'.

Reducing the daily motion, the 12° 24' become 744'. Dividing the 744 by the daily increment, 15', gives 50' travel by the Moon for each 1' increment. At noon March 15, 1920, the Moon lacks 5° 07', or 307' of entering the sign Aquarius. Dividing 307 by 50 gives the increment at the time the Moon enters Aquarius as 6' more than its increment at noon. As we want the increment midway between noon and this position we divide the 6 by 2 and it gives 3'. Adding this 3' to the 12° 16' travel at noon gives the average travel for the 5° 07' as 12° 19'.

(a) is 12° 19', or 739'.

(b) is 5° 07', or 307'.

(c) is 24h, or 1440m.

By proportion, multiplying (b) 307 by (c) 1440 gives 442080. Dividing 442080 by (a) 739 gives (d) 598' or 9h 58'. By logarithms, subtracting log. (a) .2897 from log. (b) .6712 gives .3815, which is the log. of (d) 9h 58'.

Adding the 9h 58m found by either method to noon gives Moon 00 Aquarius 00 March 15, 1920, 9:58 P.M. Greenwich time.

Solar Revolutions

A solar revolution is a chart erected for the moment the transiting Sun returns to the same sign, °, and ' of the zodiac it occupies in the birth chart. The chart should be erected for the latitude and longitude occupied by the person at that time. Our research department has not found solar revolutions reliable in indicating what will transpire during the following year. But the time of the Sun's transit thus over its birth-chart position is a creative period of value.

Example 8. For what Standard time of day at Los Angeles, California, in 1932, should the chart for a solar revolution relative to chart 317c be erected?

July 4, 1932, the ephemeris shows the Sun 12 Cancer 16, and thus lacking from the required position (b) 20'.

The daily motion of the Sun is (a) 57'.

(c) is 24h, or 1440m.

Solving the problem in the ordinary way shows that to move (b) 20' the Sun requires 8h 25m. From 8:25 P.M. Greenwich time, subtract the 8h Standard time difference of Los Angeles and it gives transiting Sun conjunction Sun *r* July 4, 1932, 0:25 P.M., Pacific Standard Time.

Lunar Revolutions

When the transiting Moon makes the conjunction with its birth-chart place is one type of lunar revolution. The other, and more creative period, is when the transiting Moon makes the conjunction with the birth-chart position of the Sun. In either, the chart should be erected for the latitude and longitude occupied by the person at that time. Our research department has not found lunar revolutions reliable in indicating what will transpire during the following month. And it has not found that the house of the birth chart occupied by the

New Moon is of more significance than ordinary transit positions. After doing a great deal of research on this matter it has found that an eclipse of Sun or Moon falling on a birth-chart luminary or other birth-chart position is of no more significance than a heavy transit.

To find the time for erecting a lunar cycle, find the time the Moon reaches the cycle position just as in calculating when an aspect is perfect, or a planet reaches a given position, as illustrated in examples 2, 3, and 4.

Diurnal Revolutions

A diurnal revolution is a chart erected for the moment the Asc. on the given day reaches the sign, °, and ' of the zodiac occupied by the Asc. in the birth chart. The chart should be erected for the latitude and longitude occupied by the person at that time. Our research department has not found diurnal revolutions reliable in indicating what will happen during the following day.

Examples of finding the time of day for which to erect a chart to give a selected sign, °, and ' on the Asc. are given on pages 162 and 164 of chapter 8 (Serial Lesson 117).

Chapter 8

Rectifying the Horoscope

Serial Lesson Number 117
Original Copyright, 1934
Elbert Benjamine
a.k.a. C. C. Zain

Copyright 2014, The Church of Light

Checking the Rectified Chart For Accuracy

The birth-chart constants of 30 different vocations are given in the reference book *How to Select a Vocation.** The birth-chart and progressed constants of 20 different events are set forth in the reference book *When and What Events Will Happen.** The birth-chart and progressed constants of 160 different diseases are given in Course 16, *Stellar Healing*. Other birth-chart and progressed constants are given in additional C. of L. Astrological Reports.

If the chart is correct it will have not only a major-progressed aspect to the ruler of the house mapping the department of life affected by the event, and the major-progressed constants of the event—often involving the rulers of several houses—at the time the event occurs, but as an additional check, the major-progressed aspect indicating the event in each case must be reinforced by a minor-progressed aspect and released by a transit aspect. Both the minor-progressed aspect and the transit aspect must be made to one of the four terminals of this major-progressed aspect.

If the ruler of the house mapping the department of life affected by the major-progressed aspect, and each of the other major-progressed constants, are not thus reinforced by a minor-progressed aspect and released by a transit aspect at the time of the event, the house positions of the chart are not correct.

Not neglecting parallel aspects, even those involving birth-chart and progressed Asc. and M.C., each such progressed aspect must be not over one degree from perfect.

*Out of print, see Astrology: 30 Years Research by Doris Chase Doane.

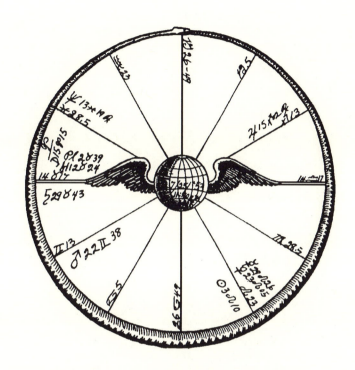

David Belasco

July 25, 1853, 11:40 p.m. L.M.T. 122½W 38N.

Famous (ruler of 10th in 1st, trine M.C.) theatrical producer Venus conjunction Mercury in 5th, house of the theatre, trine Moon, sextile Mars; Mercury trine Pluto, sextile Mars.

Abundant money from the public; Jupiter in 8th, trine Sun, trine Moon.

Dramatic ability: Neptune elevated, sextile Asc., semisextile Moon.

Originality: Uranus conjunction the Asc.

Cooperation with others. Pluto square Sun, trine Mercury.

Organization, system, perseverance: Saturn in 1st, sextile Sun.

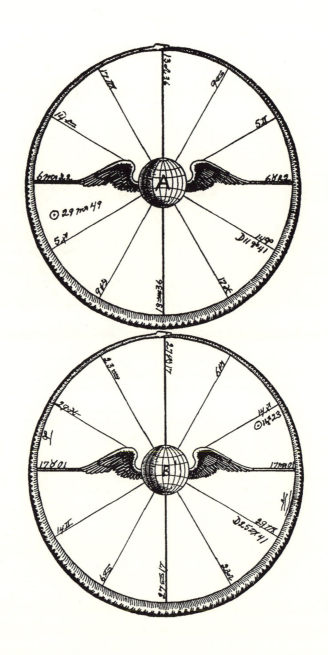

Chapter 8

Rectifying the Horoscope

A birth chart, according to the views presented in these lessons, is a map of the thought energies within the astral body of man, and the progressed aspects map the time and nature of the inner-plane weather which adds planetary energies to these thought energies. Thus natal astrology becomes a means of estimating the various forces within man's finer body at any selected time.

These forces, like any forces of nature, if left to themselves, flow on in their accustomed channels. Thus does electricity flow, and the current of a stream, or the wind through the trees. Thus also does light from the Sun beat upon our earth. Yet all of these forces have been harnessed by man and diverted from their customary channels to perform work of his choosing.

And it has been one of the objects of this series of lessons in natal astrology to indicate not merely how the energies reaching the astral body of man may accurately be estimated as to volume and their natural trend, but also to indicate the methods by which they can be controlled, diverted, and employed to do the kind of work he most desires of them.

But if such estimation of their power is to be accurate, and if the instructions as to the manner in which they can be manipulated to perform a more constructive purpose is to be sound, the birth chart which forms the basis from which these matters are judged must be accurate.

Unfortunately, many people do not know the hour of their birth. It might be held that Nature should provide a sure and easy way to remedy this negligence upon the part of man. But so far as I have been able to discover no such easy and certain method is at hand by which we can offset the ignorance of those who have failed to realize the importance of accurately timing each birth. And in this Nature seems quite consistent; for it is her custom to exact dear payment for ignorance, no matter how innocent of wrong doing it may be.

I wish there were an easy method by which, when the day of birth alone is known, a birth chart might be rectified so that the sign, degree and minute rising might be known with certainty. Yet I have experimented with "progressing the house cusps," the "noon-point method," the "sunrise method," the "tidal point method," the "octagonal point method," the "improved Egyptian method," the "pointer method," methods based upon horary charts and methods based upon the person's name, without finding in any one the precision and certainty I desire.

The magazines hold glowing advertisements of those who will rectify a birth chart by some easy and sure method. Yet I find that when a birth which is accurately timed is sent to these individuals with only the day given, that the chart returned as the correct one all too often is entirely different than the one erected for the time given by the electric clock in the maternity hospital.

There are those who boast that they never delineate a chart, even when the time of day is given, unless they first rectify it.

In our research department we have found it better always to use the time of day given. The chart thus obtained may be a few degrees in error; but we believe the error introduced by using the approximate time as ascertained by a clock by someone present at the birth, is likely to be much smaller than the error commonly occasioned in trying to make the chart fit some theory. If a birth is accurately timed I consider it a great mistake to juggle it in any way. Theories should be made to fit facts, and the observed time of birth is the fact in this case that all theories should be made to fit.

The best solution of uncertain birth times in the future is to create a public sentiment that will insure all births being accurately timed and recorded. But in the meantime those who know the day of birth, but not the hour, need not be discouraged. If enough work is done upon a chart, with the collaboration of the person to whom the chart belongs, it is possible to rectify it, that is, to experiment with it until the sign, degree and minute on the Ascendant are precisely ascertained. But the work involved, while the benefit to the individual is worth immeasurably more than the labor expended, often is so great that the professional astrologer cannot afford to give it the painstaking care that is required. His time is worth something, and he cannot, for the compensation received, afford to spend several days perhaps, experimenting with a single chart.

But the astrological student himself can well afford to experiment with his chart until he is certain it is correct. Instead of a few paltry dollars, which the professional astrologer would receive as pay, it means to him, if he takes the pains to understand his chart, a far more successful life. It may mean all the difference between success and failure. He cannot afford not to have his correct birth chart, whatever the cost to him in time and labor.

The First Step in Rectification

The first step, as a general rule, is to find the rising sign. Quite frequently, as indicated in chapter 3 (Serial Lesson 105), Course 10-1, *Delineating the Horoscope*, planets in the first house, the sign in which the planet ruling the cusp of the Ascendant is found, the Sun sign and the Dominant planet, all have some influence over the personal appearance. Therefore, while occasionally the rising sign marks the person so clearly that there can be no mistake, more frequently the combined impress of these other influences is so strong as to make judgment from the appearance given solely by the rising sign unsatisfactory.

More commonly the personal appearance should be taken as but one of a number of indices pointing to the correct birth chart. It should be used in combination with these other factors, and to do this the more that is known about the person the better. The type of fortune he has had in each department of life is significant, and when the outstanding events relating to each occurred.

When the fortune which has already been attracted relative to any particular department of life is clear cut in its trend, it signifies that a planet rules the house governing that department of life which by its Keyword and the Keyword of its aspects is characteristic of that fortune.

A house may be ruled by a planet which is not in that house, it is true. But by making inquiry in reference to the events, or conditions, that the life has experienced in relation to each of the 12 houses, with a trial chart showing the aspects before one, it often quickly becomes apparent just how the planets must fit into the various houses to produce the known effects.

This is very much like piecing together a jigsaw puzzle. And to start with, if no opinion is entertained as to the rising sign, it is well to use a Natural Chart. That is, to use a chart with no-degrees Aries on the Ascendant. This trial chart may then be manipulated, by turning it around gradually, until it reaches a place in reference to the house positions of the planets, and the planetary rulership of the houses, which fits the known facts of the life. And, like a jigsaw puzzle, when the proper relations are established, it is clear that the correct combinations have been obtained.

A Natural Chart is one with Aries on the cusp of the 1st house, with Taurus on the cusp of the 2nd house, with Gemini on the cusp of the 3rd house, and so on; with the planets inserted just as they appear in the ephemeris at Greenwich on the day of birth.

This is the best of all charts to use when the hour of birth is not even approximately known, and there is no incentive for doing the great amount of work necessary to careful rectification. That is, it is better to give judgment from such a chart than to hazard a mere guess at the rising sign.

From such a Natural Chart no attempt should be made to predict the department of life influenced by each planet. It is enough in such cases to know the general significance of the planets in a house as given in chapters 3 (Serial Lesson 47), Course 2, *Astrological Signatures* and chapter 7 (Serial Lesson 116).

Starting with such a Natural Chart, which can be copied from the ephemeris for the day of birth in a few moments, the eye should follow down the page of the ephemeris and the chief aspects that form between the planets as there shown—the Major-Progressed Aspects to the Progressed Planets—and the chief aspects that form between the planets in the ephemeris and the birth-chart planets—the Major-Progressed Aspects to birth-chart planets—noted.

Even without setting up any chart, a person of ready wit can give quite a startling demonstration of astrology from a public platform with nothing to aid him but a set of ephemerides.

He asks someone in the audience to give the day and year of his birth. This date he finds in the ephemeris and marks it with his finger.

Then he runs his eye down the column of the ephemeris, or even through several pages of it if the person receiving the reading is elderly, and picks out the more spectacular aspects between the Major-Progressed Planets, and from them to the birth-chart planets which he has marked with his finger.

Counting ahead as many years as days have passed in the ephemeris since the birth date to the day when the aspect is formed, he then tells the audience that in such a year the individual had much trouble, that there were obstacles to overcome, that there were disappointment and loss, etc. He informs those present that in another year, which he names, the individual had good fortune, that affectional matters prospered, or that fine opportunities for advancement were present.

The general nature of the planet indicates the conditions accompanying the event, and the Keyword of the aspect, as given in chapter 6 (Serial Lesson 108), Course 10-1, *Delineating the Horoscope*, indicates the nature of the fortune or misfortune attracted into the life. chapters 3, 4 and 5 (Serial Lessons 112-114) give still further information as to what is commonly attracted under each Major-Progressed Aspect to each of the ten planets.

A student quick to note aspects and count ahead the number of days that have elapsed when they occur, can thus locate the years in which many of the chief Major Progressions form temporary stellar aerials across the astral body, and do it about as fast as he can talk in giving such a reading from the rostrum.

By picking only the most pronounced Major-Progressed Aspects in each case, he can insure that the event he describes in general terms did take place within the designated year. He cannot, of course, give detail, or determine the department of life affected by the progressed aspect, as this requires that the house positions of the planets be known. But following such a method he can point out to a large number of persons in an audience during a single evening the most pronounced events of their lives, and designate the years in which they occurred.

Trial and Error

It is because events can thus be described in general terms, and in approximate dates, without house positions, that the student must carefully distinguish between the general influence commonly exerted by a planet, and the department of life affected, in the process of rectification.

The Brotherhood of Light Astrological Reports will be found of much assistance in this trial and error process of rotating the chart until the signs and planets occupy the correct houses. The Birth-Chart Constants for the various vocations may furnish valuable hints. Likewise, the Birth-Chart Constants and Progressed Constants for the diseases from which the client has suffered, as set forth in Course 16, *Stellar Healing,* may be employed.

Referring to these B. of L. Reports, we find that people marry, separate, or divorce, for instance, only when there is a Major-Progressed Aspect to the ruler of the 7th. If legal action is taken, in obtaining a divorce or in other affairs, there is a Major-Progressed Aspect at the time to the ruler of the 9th.

People lose their children through death only when there is a Major-Progressed Aspect to both the ruler of the 5th and the ruler of the 8th. Mothers die only when there is a Major-Progressed Aspect to the ruler of the 10th and another to the ruler of the 8th. Fathers die only when there is a Major-Progressed Aspect to the ruler of the 4th and to the ruler of the 8th. Brothers or sisters die only when there is a Major-Progressed Aspect to the ruler of the 3rd and to the ruler of the 8th.

People make or lose money only when there is a Major-Progressed Aspect to the ruler of the 2nd. They are ill only when there is a Major-Progressed Aspect to the ruler of the 6th and a Major-Progressed Aspect to the ruler of the 1st. They get employment, or lose it, only when there is a Major-Progressed Aspect to the ruler of the 10th and another to the ruler of the 6th.

These Progressed Constants, and others which are given in the B. of L. Astrological Reports, as well as the department of life ruled by the house which an outstanding event chiefly influences, all can be used as indices to the relation of the houses to the signs and planets in the correct birth chart

When a chart is obtained through this trial and error method that seems to be close to the correct one, each house in turn should be given due consideration as to the events that have occurred in the department of life signified, to ascertain if the planet in it, or ruling its cusp, indicates such fortune or misfortune. Likewise, the chief Major-Progressed Aspects of the planet ruling the house should be calculated to determine if the events attracted at the indicated times are such as should be expected.

Minor Progressions also are of great value to the individual who is attempting to rectify his own chart, or who is attempting to rectify the chart of some person with whom rather closely associated.

One seldom has long to wait until there is some new Minor-Progressed Aspect formed of significance enough to attract some well defined Minor Event. Such events are seldom of importance enough to be marked strongly in the memory. But as they occur they are easily observed. And, quite as much as Major Progressions, they tend to attract events that relate to the departments of life ruled by the houses which the aspecting planets rule or occupy. And as they occur so frequently, it is possible to observe enough of them within a year or so, to quite thoroughly check the accuracy of the selected birth chart.

Thus if the individual is invited to some social event where he has a particularly good time, he may look up the Minor-Progressed Aspect coincident with it. If a small debt which he never expected to be paid is collected, let him look up the Minor Progressions on that day and ascertain how they coincide as to house position in the selected chart with such collection. Or if he makes an enemy, takes a little trip, or any other of the numerous Minor Activities that make up the common run of life, let him observe how the Minor Progressions at the time, through their relation to house positions, bear out the chart he has decided upon.

Finding the Time of Day of the Trial Chart

Such a trial and error chart must have approximately some degree of some sign on the 10th house. From a Table of Houses copy the other signs and degrees upon the various house cusps that are given when this sign and degree are on the 10th. Then observe in the Table of Houses what Sidereal Time corresponds to this position of sign and degree on the cusp of the 10th. Turn to the day of birth in the ephemeris and note the Sidereal Time at Noon there given. The difference between the Sidereal Time for noon as given in the ephemeris and the Sidereal Time of birth as determined from the sign and degree and on the cusp of the 10th, gives approximately the LMT Interval from Noon on the day that birth took place.

The student should note that this Interval cannot be greater than 12 hours without passing into another day, and this is not permissible; for people usually know the day on which they were born. Consequently, when the difference appears greater than 12 hours, 24 hours should be added to the less Sidereal

Time, and the other Sidereal Time should be subtracted from it to find the Interval from Noon.

Thus suppose we have a chart for Nov. 30, 1920, with 00 Taurus 00 on the M.C. The Sidereal Time of birth is 1h 51m 37s. Now if we subtract 1h 51m 37s from 16h 36m 13s, it gives us an Interval of 14h 44m 36s. As the Noon Sidereal Time is 16h 36m 13s and we subtract this Interval to get 1h 51m 37s, it signifies that to get the time of day we must subtract 14h 44m 36s from Noon. But this carries us back into the previous day, or Nov. 29, which as the birth was on Nov. 30 is not permissible.

Instead of doing this, therefore, we add 24h to the 1h 51m 37s, giving us 25h 51m 37s. And from this we subtract the 16h 36m 13s, which gives us 9h 15m 24s. And as to the Sidereal Time at Noon we must add this 9h 15m 24s to get the Sidereal Time of Birth, we know that this Interval is After Noon. The time of birth, consequently, is Nov. 30, 1920, 9:15 p.m. LMT minus or plus the correction of 9.86 seconds per hour for EGMT Interval.

Finding the Exact Degree and Minute on the M.C.

When the student has the chart of birth as closely rectified as possible by the trial and error method, he should next endeavor to ascertain the exact degree and minute on the M.C. In this work he can apply either one or both of two methods. One is the Prenatal Epoch Method, and the other is to make use of progressions of, and progressions to, the Ascendant and Midheaven.

The method of using Major and Minor-Progressed Aspects to and from the Asc. and M.C. is feasible only when there are events in the life that cannot adequately be explained by the progressions of the planets.

Progressed aspects to the Asc. and M.C., and from the Asc. and M.C., are quite as effective in forming temporary stellar aerials which pick up energy and attract events into the life as are similar aspects to and from the planets. Consequently, if there have been strong Major-Progressed Aspects to or from these Angles in the birth chart, they should have been marked by characteristic events.

The difficulty encountered in using progressed aspects to or from the Asc. and M.C. as a basis of rectification lies in the fact that more often than might be expected there is at the same time one of these progressed aspects is in force, also a progressed aspect between planets. It is not a simple matter, by any means, to determine under such circumstances just what part in attracting the event was taken by the Asc. or M.C., and what part was taken by the Major-Progressed planets.

Yet we may be sure of this, that when the Major-Progressed Asc. or the Major-Progressed M.C makes outstanding aspects to the planets, or the

Major-Progressed planets make outstanding aspects to the Asc. or M.C., events of considerable importance enter the life. If the Asc. is involved, these relate to personal matters; but if the M.C. is part to the aspect the honor and business are affected. If it is discovered, therefore, that no such circumstances were present when these heavy progressed aspects formed in the trial chart, it is quite certain that it is not yet precisely correct.

A good method is first to compare the events of life that have occurred with the Major-Progressed Aspects of the planets at the time of each, to discern if each event is thus properly accounted for, and if not whether a progression involving the Asc. or M.C. would better account for it. With this done, take up the Major-Progressed Aspects from and to the Asc. and M.C., starting with birth and tabulating each up to the time rectification is attempted.

If the chart is correct as to the exact degree on the Asc. and M.C. the time of each progressed aspect thus tabulated will correspond to a characteristic event in the life. If events do not closely coincide with the time of these progressed aspects, the chart needs further manipulation; and in this case, if it is close to being correct, the amount of movement forward or backward required to make the Asc. and M.C. properly fit with events often is clearly indicated. As a further check, the Minor-Progressed Aspects to and from the Asc. and M.C. may be employed.

This trial and error method requires persistent work and careful checking, but if carried out thoroughly gives a chart that may be relied upon more implicitly than one rectified by any other method about which I know.

The Truitine of Hermes

Under normal conditions there seems to be an interchange of positions between the horizon at the moment of a child's conception and the place of the Moon at the moment of birth; and an interchange of positions between the place of the Moon at the moment of a child's conception and the horizon at the moment of a child's birth.

Where sympathetic relations between earth and sky are not interfered with by artificial conditions or untoward events, the degree of the zodiac on the Ascendant or Descendant at conception becomes the degree of the zodiac occupied by the Moon at birth; and the degree of the zodiac occupied by the Moon at conception becomes the degree of the zodiac on the Ascendant or Descendant at birth.

This law handed down from a remote past as the Truitine of Hermes has been amplified by modern astrologers, who have added other valuable factors. The application of this ancient law in connection with modern factors and a vast amount of detail has given rise to an elaborate theory called the Prenatal Epoch.

The Prenatal Epoch

The prenatal epoch is of great value in rectifying horoscopes, but in my opinion, which is not shared by all astrologers, is quite valueless in rectification unless the time of birth is ascertained within half an hour of the correct time by some other method.

To apply the method it is necessary to know approximately the sign and degree occupied by the Moon at conception, and to ascertain this it becomes necessary to know approximately the sign and degree on the Ascendant at birth.

The word conception as used in this connection is not coincident with any physical act, but denotes the moment when, through the union of ovum and spermatozoon, the astral body of the child to be born becomes attached to the ovum thus fertilized. In my opinion, which is not shared by all, this attachment is never previous to the physical relations of the parents. The fertilization of the ovum and the attachment of the astral form to it, however, may occur any time during several days after the union of the parents.

With the time of birth approximately known, and the number of days of gestation definitely known, it is a simple matter to calculate the time of conception closely; for the degree occupied by the Moon in the birth chart represents the degree on the horizon at that time, and the Moon must be in a degree of the zodiac not far removed from the approximately known horizon of the birth chart.

From the degree and sign on the horizon at conception the time of day at the moment of conception may readily be calculated, and from this time the degree of the Moon at conception may be ascertained, as in any birth chart. The degree of the Moon at conception, thus found, represents the exact degree on the horizon of the birth chart.

Unfortunately for the infallibility of this method, in some cases it is very difficult to determine the exact number of days of gestation.

The enthusiastic advocates of the method have formulated some very complex Laws of Sex, based upon the supposed value of the quadrants, and the supposed sex value of certain degrees of the zodiac. Unless the chart erected for the epoch—as the true moment of conception commonly is known—by the value of the area occupied by the Moon and Ascendant confirm the sex of the child, the epoch is regarded as fictitious, and an epoch for a different day is sought.

While the Truitine of Hermes certainly seems to formulate a natural law, this "Paramount Law of Sex," as it is called by its advocates, seems to me to be too artificial and theoretical to be relied upon implicitly. Yet it does deserve investigation and critical study, as it is a serious attempt, at least partially successful, to solve one of the most difficult situations met within the practice of natal astrology.

Those who wish to do so can find a full exposition of the various ramifications of the "Paramount Law of Sex," in connection with the Prenatal Epoch in a book of considerable size by E. H. Bailey, bearing the title, *The Prenatal Epoch*.

In my own investigations, and those of our research department, as near as it is possible to decide so uncertain a matter, we have found that without recourse to the "Paramount Law of Sex," when the birth time is approximately known, the birth chart may be rectified to the correct degree and minute of the rising sign by the Prenatal Epoch in about seven charts out of ten. About 30% of all charts, apparently, do not yield to the regular method of treatment, because the duration of gestation, due to instrumental deliveries, to artificial environment, or other conditions, does not conform to the regular rule.

There are rules given by Bailey for calculating these variations, but they soon lead into bewildering complexities that make them not entirely satisfactory. Consequently, unless the student has the time and inclination to give a very thorough and detailed study to the Prenatal Epoch, when he finds that rectification by the Prenatal Epoch gives a birth time beyond the probable error of observation, it is better for him to make the rectification by the other previously mentioned methods.

Whether Moon and Ascendant or Moon and Descendant Should Be Used

In applying the Prenatal Epoch the first essential knowledge is whether the interchange of places occurs between the Moon and Ascendant or between the Moon and Descendant. In determining this, as well as in determining whether the period of gestation is shorter or longer than the average, the other of the three most important birth-chart factors, the Sun, must also be considered.

RULE XIX. When in the birth chart the Moon is Increasing in light, its position is the degree on the Ascendant at the epoch, and the position of the Moon at the epoch is the degree on the Ascendant in the birth chart.

RULE XX. When in the birth chart the Moon is Decreasing in light, its position is the degree on the Descendant at the epoch, and the position of the Moon at the epoch is the degree on the Descendant in the birth chart.

RECTIFYING THE HOROSCOPE

Whether Gestation Is Shorter or Longer Than 273 Days

The average period of gestation is considered to be ten lunar months, or nine calendar months, or 273 days. To know whether the period of gestation was longer or shorter than 273 days the following rules have been formulated:

RULE XXI. When in the birth chart the Moon is Increasing in light and Below the earth, or is Decreasing in light and Above the earth, the period of gestation is more than 273 days.

RULE XXII. When in the birth chart the Moon is Increasing in light and Above the earth, or is Decreasing in light and Below the earth, the period of gestation is less than 273 days.

How Much Gestation Is Shorter or Longer Than 273 Days

To find the number of days that the period of gestation was more or less than 273 days the following two rules customarily are used:

RULE XXIII. When the period of gestation is shown to be more than the average length, find the number of degrees in the birth chart between the Moon and the Horizon to which it is approaching by the diurnal rotation of the earth, and divide this number by 13 (the average daily motion of the Moon), which will give the number of days in excess of 273 occupied by gestation.

RULE XXIV. When the period of gestation is shown to be less than the average length, find the number of degrees in the birth chart between the Moon and the Horizon last crossed by it due to the diurnal motion of the earth, and divide this number by 13 (the average daily motion of the Moon), which will give the number of days less than 273 occupied by gestation.

Theoretically, counting back in the ephemeris as many days as is indicated by the above rules, the Moon should be found in the same sign and near the exact degree occupied by the Ascendant or Descendant, as determined by the above rules, in the approximate birth chart.

Unfortunately this is not always actually the case, but is usually near a day in the ephemeris in which the Moon is in such a sign and degree, and in this case that latter day should be used. In applying the Law of Sex there is a variation to the rule given by which a still further 14 days are added to the period of gestation when it is more than 273 days, or 14 additional days are subtracted when the period of gestation is shown to be less than 273 days. Further, there are supposed to be Three Irregular Epochs that because of the Law of Sex require special treatment.

Complexities begin to multiply. I believe, however, that about seven out of every ten birth charts can be rectified by the Prenatal Epoch when the time of birth is approximately known without reference to any of these elaborate and special considerations which are not held in favor by all astrologers. Let us, therefore, apply the regular Prenatal Rules to two example charts:

Example 1. A child was born in New York City, November 22, 1920, at approximately 5:00 a.m., Local Mean Time. What was the exact degree and minute rising at the true moment of birth?

First we erect a trial chart for the time of birth, inserting only the Sun and Moon (Diagram A at front of this chapter).

As the Moon is Increasing in light—moving toward the opposition with the Sun—the place of the Moon in the birth chart, 11 Aries 41, is the Ascendant at the epoch (Rule XIX). Also (Rule XXI) the period of gestation is more than 273 days.

From 6 Scorpio to 12 Aries is 156 degrees. Divide this by 13 and it gives 12 days more than 273 as the period of gestation (Rule XXIII).

Counting back 9 calendar months brings us to Feb. 22; and as we desire to find 273 days, or 10 lunar months, we look to see on what date near this day the Moon is in 12 Aries, as at birth. This is Feb. 23, 1920.

Counting 12 days back from Feb. 23 gives us Feb. 11. Here we find the Moon in 17 Scorpio. But as we have reason to believe the birth was timed within half an hour or less of being correct, we drop back another day to Feb. 10, with the Moon in 5 Scorpio 28. This then is one of the many cases in which the rule for finding the length of gestation brings us close to the correct day but does not give us the exact day.

As the Ascendant on this day of conception, or Epoch, was the place of the Moon in the birth chart, we must find at what time 11 Aries 41 was on the Ascendant on Feb. 10, 1920. The Table of Houses for New York shows that when 11 Aries 41 is on the Ascendant the Sidereal Time is 18h 27m 00s. The Sidereal Time at noon on Feb. 10 was 21h 17m 06s. Subtracting 18h 27m 00s from 21h 17m 06s gives an Interval of 2h 50m 06s before noon. To this add the correction of 9.86s per hour for the plus 2h 06m EGMT Interval (equivalent to subtracting it from the S.T.) and it gives 2h 50m 27s as the minus LMT Interval of the Epoch at New York. This means 9:10 a.m. LMT New York or plus 2h 06m EGMT Interval on Feb. 10, 1920.

The place of the Moon on Feb. 10, at plus EGMT Interval 2h 06m (9:10 a.m. LMT New York) is found to be 6 Scorpio 31. Therefore 6 Scorpio 31 was on the Ascendant at birth.

The Table of Houses for New York shows that when 6 Scorpio 31 is on the Ascendant the Sidereal Time is 9h 05m 07s. The Sidereal Time at noon on November 22, 1920, is 16h 04m 40s. Subtracting 9h 05m 07s from 16h 04m 40s gives an Interval of 6h 59m 33s before noon. From this subtract the correction of 9.86s per hour for the minus 2h 04m EGMT Interval and it gives minus 6h 59m 12s LMT Interval. Subtracting this from noon gives the LMT time of birth at New York as 5:01 a.m.

Example 2. A child was born in New York City, December 3, 1920, at 3:08 p.m., Local Mean Time. What was the exact degree and minute on the Ascendant at the true moment of birth?

First we erect a trial chart inserting the Sun and Moon only (Diagram B at the front of this chapter).

In this chart for the time given the Moon is seen to be Decreasing in light—going toward the conjunction with the Sun. Therefore (Rule XX), the position of the Moon at birth, 25 Virgo 41, was the Descendant at conception. Also (Rule XXII), the period of gestation was less than 273 days.

Applying Rule XXIV, from 26 Virgo to 17 Scorpio is 51 degrees. Divide the 51 by 13 and it gives 4 as the number of days the period of gestation was less than 273 days.

Going back in the ephemeris 9 calendar months and looking for a day close to this time that shows the Moon again in 26 Virgo, we come to March 5, 1920. However, as seen, the period of gestation was 4 days less than this average time, so we come to March 9 as the day of the Epoch.

Next we desire to know the time of day at New York when 25 Virgo 41 was on the Descendant, which is the same as when 25 Pisces 41 is on the Ascendant.

A Table of Houses for New York shows us that when 25 Pisces 41 is on the Ascendant the Sidereal Time is 17h 50m 05s. The Sidereal Time at noon on March 9, 1920, was 23h 07m 29s. Subtracting 17h 50m 05s from 23h 07m 29s gives us an Interval of 5h 17m 24s. From this subtract the correction of 9.86s per hour for the minus 21m EGMT Interval and it gives us 5h 17m 20s as the minus LMT Interval of the Epoch at New York. This means 6:43 a.m. LMT New York or 11:39 a.m. Greenwich, March 5, 1920.

Then we calculate the position of the Moon on March 9, 1920, at 11:39 a.m. Greenwich and find it was 13 Scorpio 01. Therefore, in the birth chart 13 Scorpio 01 was on the Descendant, which gives 13 Taurus 01 on the Ascendant at the true moment of birth.

The Table of Houses for New York shows that when 13 Taurus 01 is on the Ascendant the Sidereal Time is 19h 45m 55s. The Sidereal Time at noon on December 3, 1920, is 16h 48m 02s. Subtracting 16h 48m 02s from 19h 45m 55s gives an interval of 2h 57m 53s after noon. From this subtract the correction of 9.86s per hour for the plus 7h 54m EGMT Interval, and it gives 2h 56m 35s as the plus LMT Interval. This gives the LMT time of birth at New York as 2:57 p.m.

It will be seen from the above two typical examples that rectification by the Prenatal Epoch, except when unusual conditions are present, offers no greater mathematical difficulties than are ordinarily present in the erection of a birth chart.

Occasionally a birth is encountered which does not yield to the simple rules illustrated above, and then the astrologer's resourcefulness may be taxed to the limit. In these complex cases results are more satisfactory if other methods than the Prenatal Epoch be used to check the accuracy of the birth chart obtained.

Responsibility of the Astrologer to His Client

Telling the fortune of his client plays a very small part in the work of a reputable astrologer. Instead, his work largely consists in a careful appraisal of the possibilities open to his client as revealed by a study of his birth chart and the progressed aspects, and in offering advice and instructions that will enable him to take the utmost advantage of such possibilities.

There may be, and often are, conditions arising from the trend of national events and the activities and fortunes of other people, over which the individual has no control. And if he is informed of the nature of these events, when they will happen, and the bearing they will have upon his life, it will give him a certain advantage. With this knowledge he is able to shape his affairs in advance to conform to these conditions as they present themselves.

Yet the astrologer should be at some pains to impress upon him that most events affecting his life are not inevitable. They are attracted to him only because he has within his astral body thought-cells organized in a definite manner. It lies within his power to change the thought organization of his astral body, and to divert the energy of progressed aspects into channels that will enable only such groups of thought cells as he chooses to become more than normally active.

The birth chart should be viewed by the astrologer as mapping the natural tendencies and qualifications with which the individual was born. It is a map of the effect of previous experiences of the soul. It is not a map of unchanging conditions, but merely of the character, and power to attract conditions, as they exist at birth.

Yet even so, it reveals the raw materials, so to speak, with which the life begins. From it the astrologer should be able to discern the avenues of endeavor which will yield the most satisfactory results from effort expended. And he should advise his client and instruct him how to proceed, utilizing the raw materials he has, to make the most of his life.

From the birth chart the astrologer thus should analyze each department of life, and discern the normal trend of the events attracted as they relate to each of these twelve departments. This information not only should be used, as indicated, to determine the line of effort into which the energies should be directed to make the most progress, but also as a basis for advice which should be given the client on how to remodel the thought organizations in the discordant departments of life so that they will cease to attract misfortune.

Progressed aspects should not be regarded as implying inevitable events, but as temporary stellar aerials stretching across the astral body that pick up, radio fashion, new energy, which if not manipulated by the individual, is added to the thought cells in his astral body at their terminals.

If the thought cells, working from the inner plane, are to accomplish much, that is, if they are to attract events of consequence, they must be supplied with energy. Any progressed aspect maps an aerial that supplies additional energy and thus enables the thought cells of the astral body to do more work. They can attract events of an importance comparable to the amount of energy thus reaching them. Any progressed aspect, therefore, offers possibilities for attracting events that otherwise would not be present.

The problem is, not to prevent the energy picked up by even a discordant temporary stellar aerial from reaching the astral body, but so to divert, manipulate, or control it that the resulting activity of the thought cells it reaches will be harmonious enough to attract fortunate events instead of disaster.

Even the most discordant temporary energy added to thought cells in the astral body which, as shown by powerfully fortunate aspects of the planets mapping them in the birth chart, are themselves basically fortunate, is not difficult to divert, by the mental attitude or by harmonious Rallying Forces which may be present, into channels that will attract considerable good fortune. The astrologer should thus not be hasty to discourage effort under such conditions; but rather make a careful analysis of how advantage may be taken of the additional energy.

A more difficult problem is when, from the birth chart and progressed aspect, it is clear that the energy if left to itself will attract misfortune. But even in such cases possibilities are open for changing the quality of the new energy through the mental attitude. Just what those possibilities are, and to what extent his client should as completely as possible avoid certain activities and certain kinds of environment, requires keen judgment upon the part of the astrologer.

As the harmony or discord of the thought cells determines the fortune or misfortune of the event attracted, to the extent the thought cells in a given department of life are given greater harmony, to that extent are the events attracted more fortunate. Such harmony can be imparted either through the proper application of a Mental Antidote, or through Conversion, in either method the composition of the thought cells being changed; or through the application of harmonious Rallying Forces, by which process harmonious energies are so completely tuned in on that they reach all temporary stellar aerials mapped by progressed aspects at the time, and thus find their way to the stellar cells governing various departments of life.

It thus becomes the work of the astrologer, among other things, to appraise the possibilities offered by progressed aspects, and to instruct his client how the thought structure of his astral body can be changed, and the new energies mapped by progressed aspects manipulated to the best advantage.

Life presents a series of problems to each individual, and the astrologer should be an expert in assisting people, with his knowledge of astrology and the working of the unconscious mind, to solve these problems in the most advantageous manner. There is a best course of action and a best mental attitude under any condition that may arise; and it is the function of the astrologer to discover these for his client, and to make them plain to him.

When pointing out to his client the trend of developing conditions which make a course of action and mental attitude advisable, he should ever bear in mind the power of suggestion. Instead of instilling the feeling of fear, he should point out the path of constructive endeavor. His outlook should be that something always can be done, even under the most adverse conditions, to make them better than they otherwise would be.

To the extent the astrologer is able to assist people, through his advice, to overcome the limitations otherwise imposed by their birth charts, to escape the afflictions otherwise attracted by the temporary stellar aerials mapped by progressed aspects, and to attain usefulness, happiness and spirituality, is he justified in considering himself successful in his calling.

Thus will he assist others, as well as himself, to CONTRIBUTE THEIR UTMOST TO UNIVERSAL WELFARE.

Study Questions

These questions do not represent the final exam for this course.
The following questions are for study purposes only.

Note: There is only one final examination sheet for the two sections of Course 10.

Chapter 1
Hermetic System of Progressions

1. What gave the Chaldeans unusual precision in predicting?

2. Why is it best to master one system before taking up others?

3. What is lacking when Minor Progressions are neglected?

4. Why do many people tend to exaggerate the power of Transits?

5. How should the value of the three types of progressions be checked?

6. Why should all unnecessary factors be neglected?

7. Why is it possible for certain individuals, no matter what system is followed so long as it presents many factors, to get startlingly precise results?

8. Predicting depends upon ascertaining what in relation to definite groups of thought cells within the astral body?

9. As velocities increase what happens to time?

10. How long does it require for the occurrences that take place in 24 hours of the very slow Major Progression Time to express in the fast Calendar Time of the external world?

11. How long does it require for the occurrences that take place in 27.3 days (one astrological month) of the moderately slow Minor Progression Time to express in the fast Calendar Time of the external world?

12. How long does it require for the occurrences that take place in 365,b days (one year) of the fast Transit time to express in the fast Calendar time of the external world?

13. When a progressed planet forms an aspect with a planet in the birth chart, or with another major-progressed planet, what does this energy release build across the astral body?

14. What is the effective orb within which the event indicated by a progressed aspect by major, minor or transit progression may be expected to take place?

15. At one degree from perfect, about what proportion of the peak load is picked up by a progressed aspect?

16. On what does the importance of the event indicated by a progression depend?

17. What determines whether the temporary aerial mapped by a progressed aspect will give the energy it picks up a harmonious turn or will load it with discordant static?

18. Upon what within the astral body does the fortune or misfortune of the event attracted depend?

19. Is the energy supplied by a temporary stellar aerial mapped by a progressed aspect commonly of more importance in determining the amount of harmony or discord which a group of thought cells feels than are the permanent aerials mapped by aspects in the chart of birth?

20. In addition to the birth chart, what are the three positive influences in an individual's life which measure releases of energy which bring structural changes in his astral body at times which can be predetermined with which an astrologer should concern himself?

21. What is the only difference in the influence exerted by a Major-Progressed Aspect, an Independent Minor-Progressed Aspect, and an Independent-Transit Aspect?

22. Is there any difference in the precise time a progressed aspect is perfect when it is calculated by logarithms than when it is calculated by proportion?

23. What is the Limiting Date?

24. What is the Major Progression Date?

25. State for each of the ten planets, three things affected when it is a chief influence involved in a progressed aspect.

Chapter 2
Major Progressions of Sun and Angles

1. What is the relation between inner-plane weather at the time a person, creature or important event is born and the inner-plane makeup of that which is then born?

2. What does the inner-plane weather mapped by a progressed aspect do to the desires of the thought cells?

3. What inner-plane power is used by the thought cells receiving additional energy through progressed aspects to attract events of the kind they desire into the life?

4. What maps the most important inner-plane weather affecting an individual at any given time?

5. Commonly how many terminals has a major-progressed aspect?

6. At the time an event occurs or a disease develops each of its major-progressed constants is always reinforced by what?

7. At the time an event occurs or a disease develops each of its major-progressed constants is always released by what?

8. What is the outside orb limit for any progressed aspect?

9. From the EGMT Interval on the day of birth for which the planets' positions were calculated how is the Limiting Date found?

10. Is the Limiting Date always in the same year as the birth?

11. In finding the Major Progression Date for any calendar year, from what date in the ephemeris is the counting started?

12. In finding the Major Progression Date should the count be for the number of years that have elapsed since birth?

13. How is the Midheaven Constant found?

14. In working major progressions why is it usually easier to use logarithms instead of direct proportion?

15. How is calendar interval converted into equivalent EGMT Interval?

16. On a given ephemeris day what logarithms are added to find how far a planet has moved by major progression?

17. How is the major, minor or transit-progressed M.C. on a given date found?

18. How is the major, minor or transit-progressed Asc. on a given date found?

19. The logarithm of what is subtracted from the logarithm of the distance the aspect is from perfect to find the logarithm of the EGMT Interval required for the planet to close the aspect?

20. When the EGMT Interval required for the planet to close the aspect is found, how is the calendar date on which the aspect is perfect ascertained?

21. Approximately how far does the Sun move in six days by major progression, and how far in a month?

22. What is the first step in finding the calendar date on which a major-progressed aspect of the Asc. to a birth chart planet is perfect?

23. How is the progressed zodiacal motion of progressed M.C. or Asc. found?

24. When the daily motion of the M.C. or Asc. and the planet has been found, how is the calendar date on which the aspect is perfect between them ascertained?

25. In using logarithms to correct the Ascendant for latitude of birth, how is the logarithm of the correction found?

Chapter 3
Major Progressions of the Moon

1. How much power does a progressed planet have in comparison with its birth-chart terminal?

2. Other than this difference in power does a birth-chart planet receiving an aspect have a different influence than when by progression it is involved in the same aspect?

3. Does the inner-plane weather mapped by each planet tend to cause the thought cells to bring into the life conditions and events characteristic of that planet?

4. What indicates whether the inner-plane weather influenced by a progressed aspect is favorable or unfavorable, and in what way?

5. What indicates the department of life which the inner-plane weather mapped by a progressed aspect will chiefly influence?

6. An individual only gets honors when there is a progressed aspect to what planet?

7. What indicates the temporary mood influenced by a progressed aspect of the Moon?

8. Discordant progressed aspects involving what planet tend most to cause errors?

9. How much good fortune is influenced by Venus inner-plane weather?

10. What two things should be done under any progressed aspect involving Mars?

11. What is the salesmanship planet?

12. What two things should be done under any progressed aspect involving Saturn?

13. What is the instrument through which changes are brought about through the influence of Uranus inner-plane weather?

14. What is promised by Neptune usually should be discounted by about what per cent?

15. Under what inner-plane weather does the individual become most sensitive to the thoughts of those on either plane?

16. About how important are the events attracted by progressed aspects made by the Moon in comparison with similar progressed aspects made by other planets?

17. How is the motion by declination of major, minor or transit-progressed M.C. or Asc found?

18. What is the first step in finding the calendar date on which a parallel aspect involving major-progressed M.C. or Asc. is perfect?

19. What is the second step in finding the calendar date on which a parallel aspect involving major-progressed M.C. or Asc. is perfect?

20. When the daily motion by declination of M.C. or Asc. on the Map. D., and the daily motion of the planet by declination on the Map. D. have been found, what method is then followed?

21. For how far ahead should be calculated all the major-progressed aspects made by the Moon?

22. Why in calculating progressed aspects made by the Moon is it advantageous to write on the chart the sign, degree, and minute, and declination of the major-progressed M.C. and major-progressed Asc. calculated for the two consecutive Map. D.'s between which the progressed Moon Calculations are to be made?

23. Thus written, how is the yearly zodiacal motion and the yearly declination motion of M.C. or Asc. found?

24. On what date is it advantageous to start calculating the major-progressed aspects of the Moon covering one year?

25. Why is it easier to calculate the major-progressed aspects of the Moon by logarithms than by proportion?

Chapter 4
Major Progressions of the Planets

1. Parallels and conjunctions involving which planets are favorable?

2. Parallels and conjunctions involving which planets are unfavorable?

3. Which aspects between any two planets are favorable?

4. Which aspects between any two planets are unfavorable?

5. Upon what depends whether the thought cells will use their psychokinetic power to bring favorable events into the life, or unfavorable events?

6. Can the thought cells of any planetary type express either constructively or destructively?

7. Why under a progressed aspect is it advisable to permit only constructive thoughts characteristic of the planets involved to enter the mind?

8. Is it the inner plane weather mapped by an aspect which determines the fortune or misfortune coincident with it?

9. About how important is the relation to the psychokinetic power of the thought cells is the influence of physical environment?

10. What algebraic sum indicates what will happen under a given progressed aspect?

11. To insure that a more fortunate event than that indicated by a progressed aspect will be attracted, what must the thought cells mapped by each of its terminals receive?

12. Under an unfavorable progressed aspect between the Sun and a negative planet what type of thoughts should be cultivated?

13. What things should receive special attention under unfavorable progressed aspects involving the Sun?

14. What things should receive special attention under unfavorable progressed aspects involving the Moon?

15. Do good ideas and valuable discoveries often arrive under an unfavorable progressed aspect involving Mercury?

16. Under an unfavorable progressed aspect involving Venus in what manner should slights from others be treated?

17. A progressed aspect involving which planet is always present when an accident takes place?

18. Under unfavorable progressed aspects involving which planet should self-indulgence, extravagance and overexpansion be avoided?

19. What thoughts should be cultivated under an unfavorable progressed aspect involving Saturn?

20. Unusually good progress can be made in astrology and the occult sciences even under an unfavorable progressed aspect involving which planet?

21. Usually good progress can be made in fiction writing, music, or dramatic work even under an unfavorable progressed aspect involving which planet?

22. What things should be avoided under an unfavorable progressed aspect involving Pluto?

23. What is the chief energy picked up under a progressed aspect involving either the M.C. or the Asc. ?

24. What thoughts and actions should be cultivated under an unfavorable progressed aspect involving the M.C. ?

25. What thoughts and actions should be cultivated under an unfavorable progressed aspect involving the Asc. ?

Chapter 5
Minor Progressions of Sun and Angles

1. What are the two distinct influences exerted by minor-progressed aspects?

2. How much power, relative to a similar major-progressed aspect, has an independent minor-progressed aspect?

3. With what progressed aspects do minor events coincide?

4. For a major-progressed aspect to gain enough power to attract a major event in what way must it be reinforced?

5. In addition to the minor-progressed aspect to one of its terminals, what other progressed aspect in addition to the major-progressed aspect must be present at the time the event enters the life?

6. Why on certain occasions is it essential to be able to determine quite precisely when a minor-progressed aspect is, and when it is not, within the one degree of effective orb to a birth chart or a major-progressed position?

7. How do minor-progressed aspects aid in rectifying charts?

8. How do minor-progressed aspects aid in selecting the best time for doing things?

9. Are minor-progressed aspects made to other minor-progressed planets of any significance?

STUDY QUESTIONS

10. What is the Solar Constant?

11. How is the Solar Constant found?

12. What is the Minor Progression Date?

13. How is the Minor Progression Date found?

14. What is the Minor Ephemeris Date?

15. How is the Minor Ephemeris Date found?

16. How is the Minor-Progressed Position of the planets found on a given calendar date?

17. How is the calendar date found on which a minor-progressed aspect to a birth-chart or major-progressed position is perfect?

18. How is the calendar date found from Minor-Progressed M.C.?

19. How is the zodiacal motion of Minor-Progressed M.C. or Asc. found?

20. How is the sign on the M.C. found for a given Asc. ?

21. How is the calendar date found on which an aspect from minor-progressed M.C. or Asc. to a major-progressed or birth-chart position is perfect?

22. How is the declination of minor-progressed M.C. or Asc. found for a given calendar date?

23. How is the motion by declination of minor-progressed M.C. or Asc. found?

24. How is the calendar date found on which a major, minor, or transit-progressed planet, progressed M.C. or progressed Asc. reaches a given sign, degree, and minute, of the zodiac, or reaches a given degree and minute of declination?

25. How is the calendar date found on which the minor-progressed M.C. or Asc. makes a parallel aspect with a major-progressed or birth-chart position?

Chapter 6
Minor Progressions of Moon and Planets

1. Does the harmony or discord of a minor-progressed aspect to a major-progressed terminal have an appreciable effect upon the harmony or discord of the event then attracted?

2. Is it easy to determine how favorable or unfavorable the event will be which is brought to pass by a major-progressed aspect?

3. A fair estimate of what may be had by the reinforced peaks of power of a major-progressed aspect?

4. To what extent must the harmony or discord of the two planets at birth be considered when estimating how favorable or unfavorable the events will be, attracted by a major-progressed aspect involving these two planets?

5. Why does a single major-progressed aspect sometimes bring loss in one department of life, and gain in another?

6. Under what conditions is it possible for a progressed trine to bring misfortune into the life?

7. Under what conditions is it possible for a progressed square to bring good fortune into the life?

8. What calculations indicate the benefit or detriment to be expected from each department of life influenced by a progressed aspect?

9. What thing of advantage does an individual have under his command while he is under a favorable progressed aspect involving the Sun?

10. In what way can this be used as a favorable Rallying Force?

11. Only under what conditions do energies from the planets become Rallying Forces?

12. Why can progressed aspects made by the Moon so frequently be used as favorable Rallying Forces?

13. Favorable progressions involving Mercury give facility for what?

14. What attitude toward others is best under a favorable progressed aspect involving Venus?

15. Even under a favorable progressed aspect involving Mars is it always possible to avoid antagonism.

16. What is the one thing, and one thing only, needed under a favorable progressed aspect involving Mars?

17. Under a favorable progressed aspect Jupiter no effort should be spared to do what?

18. Under favorable progressed aspects involving what planet may purchases be made to best advantage?

19. Even under a favorable progressed aspect involving Saturn what thoughts need cultivation?

20. Are the attachments formed even under a favorable progressed aspect involving Uranus usually lasting?

21. What is one of the best of all progressed aspects to aid true spiritual progress?

22. Even under a favorable progressed aspect involving Pluto should an individual for a moment surrender control of himself?

23. What should be done under a favorable progressed aspect involving the M.C.?

24. What should be done under a favorable progressed aspect involving the Asc.?

STUDY QUESTIONS 177

25. How may minor-progressed aspects be calculated with a precision of less than half an hour of calendar time?

Chapter 7
Transits, Revolutions and Cycles

1. Does a major event ever take place except when a characteristic major-progressed aspect is reinforced by a minor-progressed aspect, and released by a transit-progressed aspect to one of the terminals of the major-progressed aspect?

2. What are the two distinct influences exerted by transit aspects?

3. In comparison to major-progressed aspects how much power have transit-progressed aspects?

4. Why do those who ignore major-progressed aspects, on an average miss one-half the significant transit aspects?

5. How does knowledge of the significant function of transit-progressed aspects assist in rectifying birth charts?

6. Do transit aspects of M.C. and Asc. to birth-chart and major-progressed positions exert the trigger effect?

7. Do parallel aspects of planets, M.C. and Asc. have the trigger effect?

8. Only to what positions do transit aspects have value?

9. Through what people do the astrological discords affecting nations and the world commonly operate?

10. Illustrate how a progressed aspect that would have little influence under ordinary conditions may have a drastic influence under different environmental conditions?

11. Because a major-progressed aspect has been within the one degree of effective orb for years without attracting an event, does this signify it will not eventually bring about an event characteristic of it?

12. In giving a reading, why is it so necessary to consider the power of suggestion?

13. How is the transit-progressed position of a planet found for any time of day on any calendar day?

14. How is the calendar date and time of day determined when a progressed transit aspect is perfect?

15. How is the transit-progressed M.C. found on a given date?

16. How is the transit-progressed Asc. found on a given date?

17. How is the calendar date ascertained from the transit-progressed M.C. ?

18. How is the zodiacal motion of transit-progressed M.C.? or Asc. found?

19. How is the calendar date on which a transit-progressed aspect is perfect to a birth-chart or major-progressed position found?

20. How is the declination of transit-progressed M.C. or Asc. found for a given date?

21. How is the motion by declination of transit-progressed M.C. or Asc. found?

22. How is the time of day an aspect in the sky is perfect, or a planet reaches a given sign, degree and minute of longitude, or a given degree and minute of declination ascertained?

23. Have solar revolutions been found reliable in predicting what will happen during the following year?

24. Have lunar revolutions been found reliable in predicting what will happen during the following month?

25. Have diurnal revolutions been found reliable in predicting what will happen during the following day?

Chapter 8
Rectifying the Horoscope

1. In what manner are the planetary energies added to the finer body of man subject to the same control as other forces in nature?

2. Of even greater importance, therefore, than estimating the volume and natural trend of astrological forces, as revealed astrologically, is what knowledge?

3. Why is it so important to have the correct birth chart of an individual?

4. Is there any easy and certain method to determine the correct birth chart when the hour of birth has not been noted?

5. Why is too much rectifying of birth charts, when the time of birth has been noted, bad practice?

6. What is the best solution of uncertain birth times in the future?

7. Why do professional astrologers often fail to ascertain the correct time of birth when no approximate hour has been given?

8. Why can the individual, better than the professional astrologer, afford to do sufficient work to rectify his chart beyond doubt?

9. What is the first step in rectification?

10. Why should the personal appearance be taken as only one indication of the correct rising sign?

11. What is the principle involved in revolving the chart until the houses fit the known events?

12. What is meant by a Natural Chart?

STUDY QUESTIONS

13. Why, from a Natural Chart, or any other chart in which the house positions are not known, should no attempt be made to predict the department of life affected by a progressed aspect?

14. How, without erecting a chart, can a person of ready wit give a startling demonstration of astrology from a public platform?

15. In the trial and error work of determining the correct house positions for a chart, when hour of birth is unknown, how can astrological research be used to advantage?

16. How can Minor Progressions be used by a person who is endeavoring to rectify his own chart?

17. When a chart is ascertained which is believed to be correct, how is the hour of day of birth ascertained?

18. What is the Truitine of Hermes?

19. How does the Prenatal Epoch method differ from the Truitine of Hermes?

20. When the hour of birth is approximately known, what percentage of charts can be rectified to the exact degree and minute on the Asc. by the Prenatal Epoch?

21. What should the student do when he finds that rectification of some particular chart by the Prenatal Epoch gives a birth time beyond the probable error of observation?

22. Instead of telling the fortune of the client, what constitutes the chief work of a reputable astrologer?

23. Why should the astrologer impress upon his client that the events which may affect his client's life are not inevitable?

24. In talking to his client why should the astrologer take into consideration the power of his thoughts and the power of suggestion?

25. By what standard should the astrologer measure the success of his calling?

Note: There is only one final examination on the two Sections of Course 10.

23 BOOKS
21 COURSES

BROTHERHOOD of LIGHT LESSONS

www.light.org

800 500 0453